Reinhold Ebertin
THE ANNUAL DIAGRAM

REINHOLD EBERTIN

THE ANNUAL DIAGRAM

as an Aid in Life

A Preview based on the Graphic 45° Ephemerides

Translated by

Linda Kratzsch

EBERTIN – VERLAG, D 7080 AALEN
1973

This edition was wholly produced and printed by **Ebertin—Verlag, Reinhold Ebertin,**
D 7080 Aalen/Württ., Federal Republic of Germany

INDEX

EXPLANATIONS

Symbols of the heavenly bodies:

⊙ = Sun   ☽ = Moon   ☿ = Mercury
♀ = Venus   ♂ = Mars   ♃ = Jupiter
♄ = Saturn   ♅ = Uranus   ♆ = Neptune
♇ = Pluto   ☊ = Moon's Node
M = MC = Medium Coeli   A = AS = Ascendant

Aspects:

☌ = Conjunction   (0°)   ☍ = Opposition   (180°)
□ = Square   (90°)   ∠ = Semisquare   (45°)
⊡ = Sesquisquare   (135°)

Symbols used in the Graphique Ephemerides:

Ⓥ =   Full Moon   Ⓝ =   New Moon

Ⓔ =   Eclipse of the Sun   Ⓔ =   Eclipse of the Moon

——————   movements of the planets
- - - - - - -   halfsums of the moving planets
xxxxxxxx   movement of the Moon's Node
o   passage of a transiting planet from one sign into another

On the lines of the Sun, the planets, and the Moon's Node are the symbols and the signs through which they are moving.

6

PREFACE

My book on the "Transits", subtitled "What Day Is Favorable for Me? ", was first published forty years ago and has since then been reprinted in numerous editions. It is the steady companion of many - to the extent that the wornout copy has to be replaced by a new one many times over. The book's contents are still as up-to-date now as on first publication. Nonetheless, the setting up of an annual diagram can be rendered much more easily today.

The word "transit" means a "crossing over", that is to say, the passage of the stellar bodies in motion over the sensitive points of the cosmogram (or horoscope), namely, the positions of the stellar bodies, the points of Midheaven and Ascendant, and the angular relationships, i.e. aspects of these points. In practice, this means taking up the natal chart and the ephemeris containing the daily stellar positions and checking these day by day to see which transiting stellar bodies are crossing over the individual points in the cosmogram.

The symbol we use for the transiting bodies is a "t"; an "r" is the designation for the positions as marked in the natal chart. According to custom, the natal chart, from which all calculations are derived, was known as the radix (root) horoscope or simply radix, and hence the "r".

Therefore, when we say Jupiter t = Sun r, we mean that Jupiter is currently missing the natal Sun. We avoid the terms astrology and horoscope, since today they are generally misunderstood and misinterpreted: the misusage of these concepts is extant in the daily press with its solar astrology and weekly horoscopes. For this reason, we speak of cosmobiology, meaning the correlation between the cosmic processes and living creatures, as well as earthly events. However, we do not maintain that the stellar bodies alone exercise an influence, but rather, heredity, environment, parental home, vocation, the times in which he lives, etc. also have a decisive effect on the individual.

As we have learned from recent research, which was purely cosmobiological and not astrological, the electro-magnetic fields in the solar universe have to be considered as the transmitters of "information". This information is altered by the direct influence of the stellar bodies, and these changes in turn influence brain activity, the stimulation of the nerve cells, the heart—beat, etc. This was already reported on in our journal, "Kosmobiologie", and **Dr. Fidelsberger** gave a summation of these new perceptions at the 21st Work Congress for Cosmobiological Research, in Aalen 1969. This new knowledge is primarily based on the research work undertaken by the Russian scholar **Alexander Pressmann.**

The term cosmogram designates any sort of record made of the stellar configurations not only of births, but also of events, whereas the term horoscope is generally taken to mean only the natal chart, and often, not even that: for the daily press, the solar position alone is the same as horoscope, without consideration of the other stellar bodies.

By transit, therefore, we mean a crossing point which arises when a planet in motion passes over a particular point in the cosmogram.

The Graphic 45° Ephemeris gives us a quick and easy, readable picture of an entire year and enables us to ascertain when positive or negative reaction points make their appearance, corresponding to either good or bad periods in life, to health or illness, to success or failure, or to harmony or disharmony.

THE 45-DEGREE SYSTEM

The 90° circle was introduced in Germany almost fifty years ago. In it, the signs Aries, Cancer, Libra, and Capricorn are to be found from 0 to 30°, the signs Taurus, Leo, Scorpio, Aquarius in 30° - 60°, and the signs Gemini, Virgo, Sagittarius, and Pisces are in 60°- 90°. The advantage of this is that in this system all the stellar bodies forming a conjunction, square and opposition are located in the same place, and opposite to them are the bodies in semisquare and sesquiquadrate. Therefore, it is not necessary to look up all the aspects in the cosmogram, but rather, only those points showing an aspect divisible by 90°, which will all be found together.

This system does not contain the sextiles, aspects of 60°, or the trines, aspects of 120°. Traditional astrology often considers the sextiles and trines as favorable and the other aspects as unfavorable. This has proved to be false. Even forty years ago, I pointed out the fact that sextiles and trines are aspects that correspond to a condition or state, while conjunctions, squares, and oppositions indicate a certain degree of tension or potential, and when they appear as transits, something happens, a situation is triggered. There is substantiation, too, for the predominance of such "aspects of potential" in the cosmograms of prominent or successful individuals, whereas the sextiles and trines are more in evidence in the cosmograms of everyday persons, of those who do not stand out in the crowd. It has also been found that recognition, advancement, and success are signalled by aspects of 45° and 135°.

Fig. 1 shows the "aspects of potential". For instance, when the Sun is at 10° Cancer, the aspect points or "reaction points" are to be found at 25° Leo (45°), 10° Libra (90°), 25° Scorpio (135°), 10° Aries (90°) or 25° Taurus (45°). Therefore, if a transiting planet is located at these points, it enters into relationship with the natal Sun, the result is some reaction the character of which is determined by the nature of the triggering body.

The aspects named are derived from the progressive division of the circle (into halves, quarters, eighths). This same system is for example also used for the meteorological wind rose, a diagrammatical representation of the winds and directions. The number eight has since prehistoric times been considered as a symbol for regularity and symmetry.

During the last World War, I developed the combined chart form, which contains the customary zodiacal circle with the twelve signs and the division into degrees, but surrounding this is the 90° circle. On looking at the cosmogram of President Richard Nixon, we find the Sun in the inner circle at 19°

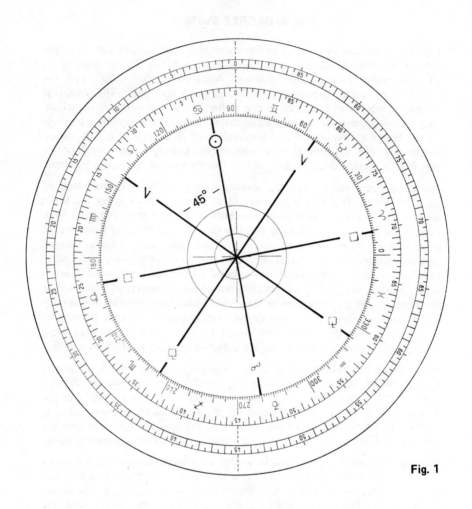

Fig. 1

K 3   Entwurf: Ing. Stefano Szaniszlo, Neapel
© Copyright 1972 Ebertin-Verlag, D-7080 Aalen

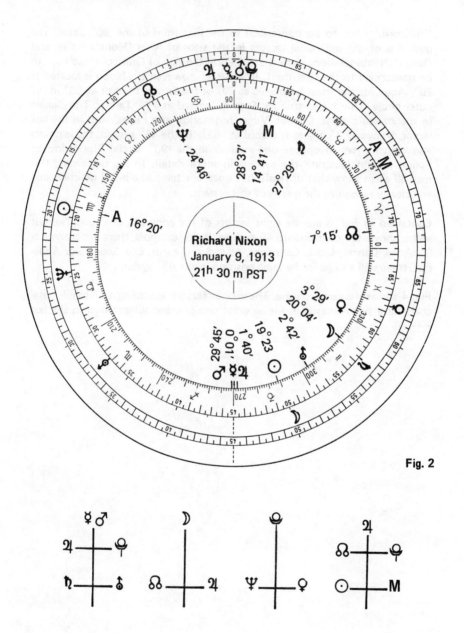

Fig. 2

11

Capricorn. It has to be transcribed to the first third of the $90°$ circle. The positions of the individual factors in the signs of Aries (Moon's Node) and Cancer (Neptune) along with the planets in the sign of Capricorn also have to be transcribed to the first third. In contrast, however, the Moon is located at $20°$ Aquarius and must be placed at $20°$ of the second third or at $50°$ in the outer circle. This is also true for Saturn, located at $27°$ Taurus. The planets in the mutable signs, Gemini, Virgo, Sagittarius, and Pisces, land in the last sector. Venus at $3°$ Pisces is placed at $63°$. In the $45°$ system, those points also coincide which oppose one another in the $90°$ circle. The following figures should illustrate the system in more detail. In the beginning, this may all seem somewhat difficult, but once one has had a bit of practice, one will clearly recognize the merits of this system.

Contained in Fig. 3 are the eight sectors of the zodiac in one row. The last sector shows the division into 45 degrees. If, for example, there are planets at $0°$ Aries, Cancer, Libra, Capricorn, or at $15°$ Taurus, Leo, Scorpio or Aquarius, these will also be in the same position in the $45°$ system.

Fig. 4 shows the same scheme. The various factors according to Nixon's natal chart have been entered in the separate sections and summarized in the last column.

Fig. 3

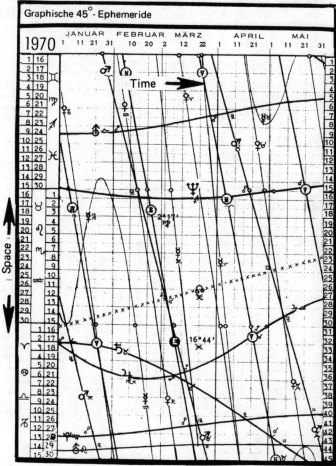

Fig. 5

13

SCHEME TO TRANSPOSE POSITIONS OUT OF THE 360° CIRCLE INTO THE 45° SCALE.

360° circle								45° scale
0°♈	15°♉	0°♋	15°♌	0°♎	15°♏	0°♑ ☿	15°♒	0°
1	16	1	16	1	16	1 ♃	16	1 ☿
2	17	2	17	2	17	2	17	2 ♃
3	18	3	18	3	18	3	18	3
4	19	4	19	4	19	4	19	4
5	20	5	20	5	20	5	20 ☾	5 ☾
6	21	6	21	6	21	6	21	6
7 ☊	22	7	22	7	22	7	22	7 ☊
8	23	8	23	8	23	8	23	8
9	24	9	24	9	24	9	24	9
10	25	10	25	10	25	10	25	10
11	26	11	26	11	26	11	26	11
12	27 ♄	12	27	12	27	12	27	12 ♄
13	28	13	28	13	28	13	28	13
14	29	14	29	14	29	14	29	14
15	0 ♊	15	0 ♍	15	0 ♐	15	0 ♓	15
16	1	16	1	16	1	16	1	16
17	2	17	2	17	2	17	2	17
18	3	18	3	18	3	18	3	18
19	4	19	4	19	4	19	4 ♀	19 ♀
20	5	20	5	20	5	20 ☉	5	20 ☉
21	6	21	6	21	6	21	6	21
22	7	22	7	22	7	22	7	22
23	8	23	8	23	8	23	8	23
24	9	24	9	24	9	24	9	24
25	10	25 ♆	10	25	10	25	10	25 ♆
26	11	26	11	26	11	26	11	26
27	12	27	12	27	12	27	12	27
28	13	28	13	28	13	28	13	28
29	14	29	14	29	14	29	14	29
0 ♉	15 M	0 ♌	15	0 ♏	15	0 ♒	15	30 M
1	16	1	16 A	1	16	1	16	31 A
2	17	2	17	2	17	2	17	32
3	18	3	18	3	18	3 ♅	18	33 ♅
4	19	4	19	4	19	4	19	34
5	20	5	20	5	20	5	20	35
6	21	6	21	6	21	6	21	36
7	22	7	22	7	22	7	22	37
8	23	8	23	8	23	8	23	38
9	24	9	24	9	24	9	24	39
10	25	10	25	10	25	10	25	40
11	26	11	26	11	26	11	26	41
12	27	12	27	12	27	12	27	42
13	28	13	28	13	28	13	28	43
14	29 ♇	14	29	14	29	14	29	44 ♇
15	0 ♋	15	0 ♎	15	0 ♑ ♂	15	0 ♈	45 ♂

Fig. 4

GRAPHIC 45° EPHEMERIS

An excerpt from the Graphic 45° Ephemeris for 1970 is reproduced in Fig. 5. It has as its components time and space. The time can be read from the top of the page, where we find the division of the year into months and days. A verticle line running to the bottom of the page is drawn for every 10th day.

On the righthand and lefthand sides, the graduated scales indicate the sectors of the zodiac. Three columns are given on the lefthand side to facilitate making entries. In the case of a planet located in the sign of Aries, Cancer, Libra, Capricorn, one would be concerned with the first column. For a planet in the sign of Taurus, Leo, Scorpio, or Aquarius the second column is applicable. A planet occupying the sign of Gemini, Virgo, Sagittarius, or Pisces will be entered in the third column. On the righthand side is the scale of degrees running from 0 to 45. This scale also serves as a guideline for the ruler when drawing the lines extending from one side to another.

The stellar orbits for the year in question in the 45° system are entered in the inside space. In order to make a simultaneous record of the relevant signs, these are likewise entered. At the beginning of the year, Uranus is at 9° Libra; Neptune is at 0° Sagittarius, Saturn at 2° Taurus, and Jupiter is at 0° Scorpio. At the point of commencement of these two planets we find the sign of opposition. The Jupiter and Saturn opposition was already due in December of 1969. As you may recall, an influenza epidemic was rampant, which is very typical of this opposition.

Along the solar orbit we see several small circles. When such a circle contains an N, this means New Moon; accordingly, F stands for Full Moon.* An E designates an eclipse: either an E in a white circle, meaning a lunar eclipse, or an E in a black circle, standing for a solar eclipse. The number of degrees given alongside indicates at which solar degree the eclipse is due.

The adventage of the Graphic Ephemeris is that it is in fact a pictorial representation, encompassing all configurations due. Far below, on January 21, we find that Mars forms an opposition to Pluto. At the same time, the Sun at Full Moon is square to Saturn. For this reason, a cold-wave (Sun = Saturn) and natural disasters could be expected at this time; there was a slight earthquake in Southern Germany and also a volcanic eruption on the island of New Britain. With the aid of the Graphic Ephemeris observations

* In German charts, not F, but V = Vollmond.

can be made of the many various events on earth and of natural phenomena. In the journal, "Kosmobiologie" with "Kosmischer Beobachter", a monthly forecast based on this method is presented.

When the orbits are slanted downwards, this means the stellar body is moving directly. In the case of an orbit curving towards the top, the body is apparently retrogressive, as seen from the earth. The more slanted the orbit, the faster the body is moving; the more the orbit approaches the horizontal plane, the slower the motion of the stellar body.

THE PRACTICAL APPLICATION OF THE 45° EPHEMERIS

Those who have overcome the initial difficulties will have made the discovery that it is possible to draw up an annual diagram and to produce a survey of the coming year within five to ten minutes time.

Several examples will demonstrate how to make practical application of the graphic ephemeris. Let us first take some examples from the realm of politics, some cases where the prognostication has proven true.

NIXON's ELECTION CONFIGURATION

Fig. 6 will result from the transcription of the positions in the 45° scheme according to the table given in Fig. 4 to the Graphic Ephemeris. The various crossing points have been marked, the small circles indicating positive configurations and the black dots negative ones. You will recall that at that time **Nixon** and **Hubert Humphrey** were opponents in the Presidential race. It then seemed that **Humphrey** would win, since he had the better configurations throughout the year. Nixon was especially hampered by aspects of Saturn. We see how Saturn transits the position lines of Moon's Node, Saturn, Venus, Sun, in succession, and then maintains for months the square to Neptune. The short-term Jupiter transits over Venus and Sun in July and over MC, AS and Uranus in September are poor compensation. But then there comes a turn-about. At the end of September, Uranus transits Mercury, and at the end of October, Jupiter, i.e. practically on the eve of the election, on November 5/6. In the bottom part of the ephemeris we find Jupiter transiting Pluto and Mars at the beginning of November. Finally, the transits of Sun and Mars over Mercury and Jupiter - at the very top - can be added to the list, altogether quite an accumulation of positive aspects at the time of election. It is only in December that negative aspects become effective in the form of Neptune t over Saturn and Saturn t over Sun.

And now making a comparison with the final months in **Humphrey's** annual diagram, we discover that as late as October he still had a number of good Jupiter transits. However, as the day of election approaches (November 9), Jupiter, Mars and Sun cluster on the position line of Saturn below, and Saturn itself transits Sun and Neptune. This synastry allowed me to prognosticate **Nixon's** victory, and this was possible half a year before the election.

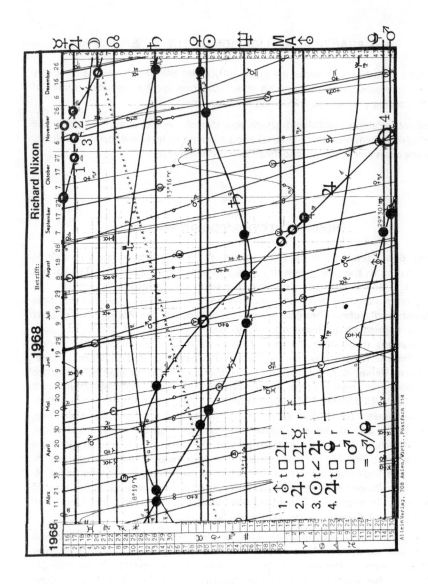

Fig. 6

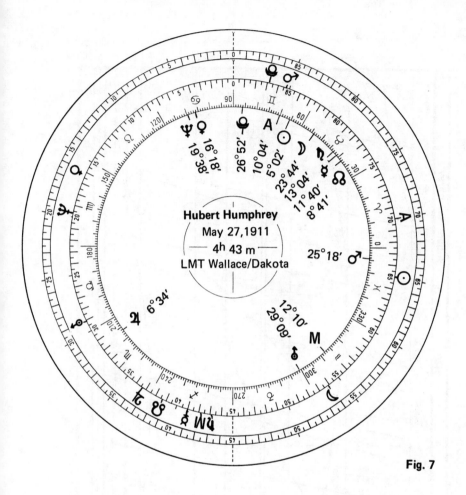

Fig. 7

19

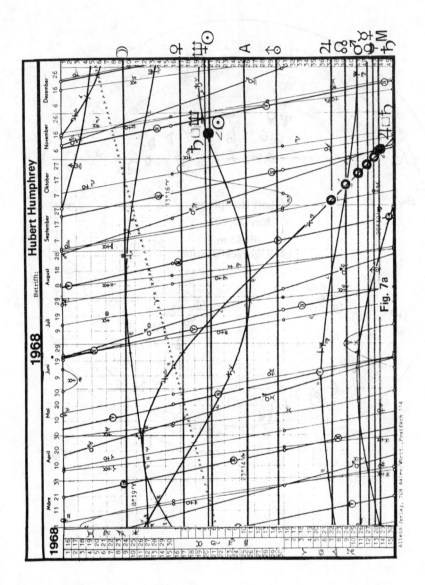

Fig. 7a

Hubert Humphrey

1968

GRAPHIC EPHEMERIS AND STRUCTURAL PICTURE

Of prime concern in the graphic 45° ephemeris are not only the transits or the reaction points, but also which cosmic condition can be attached to the transiting body or what role it plays in the structural picture. These are important factors to be taken into account when making one's interpretation.

A structural picture is obtained with the aid of the transparent calculating disc. The indicator is directed to each planet in question in the 90° circle, one then checks to see whether there are on both sides equal distances to other factors. In the case of Nixon's cosmogram (Fig. 2), we don't even need the calculating disc to recognize that at the top Mercury and Mars are located at the midpoint of Jupiter/Pluto. In addition, Mercury and Mars can also be found at Saturn/Uranus. This is in fact the really decisive success configuration in Nixon's cosmogram, since according to the CSI:

Jupiter/Pluto indicates: striving for power.

Mercury = Jupiter/Pluto: talent for speaking, desire to influence the masses - advertising campaign (here, election campaign).

Mars = Jupiter/Pluto: organizational talent, ability to enthuse others, desire to achieve great things.

This natal configuration was transited by Jupiter and Uranus. They mean:

Uranus = Jupiter/Pluto: fanatical plans for reform and innovation, quick exploitation of any situation, sudden reform, rapid development, change and transformation.

Jupiter = Jupiter/Pluto indicates the successful outcome of a striving for power, i.e. the succession to a position of power and leadership.

One important thing to remember with the graphic ephemeris is that it does not just simply end at the bottom of the page with 45°, but rather, when an orbit hits the bottom, it recommences at the top. This ephemeris must be imagined as a kind of roll on which 0° and 45° complement one another.

The conclusion to be drawn from this discussion: The transits cannot be evaluated for themselves; it is also necessary to investigate which position the transited factors take up in the natal chart.

Above, only the most important midpoints were mentioned. Mercury and Mars are also located at Saturn/Uranus, and therefore severe nervous strain and decisions under pressure are indicated. However, Jupiter's arrival at this midpoint indicates according to the CSI: happy release of tensions. This is perfectly applicable in this case in that the monthlong tension before the election finds its fortunate release in the victory.

THE ASSASSINATION OF DR. MARTIN LUTHER KING AND ROBERT KENNEDY

We have combined these two cases since they took place under similar Mars-Pluto aspects.

In the April issue of "Kosmischer Beobachter", which appeared the end of March, 1968, I pointed out the "catastrophe configuration of April 6, 1968." My words were: "Due to MA-135-PL brute force, accidents, murders are involved..." Those persons whose cosmograms contain correlations between this configuration and the individual planetary positions are most particularly endangered.

The assassination of **Dr. Martin Luther King** was already triggered on April 4, 1969, at 18 h 01 m Memphis local time. Since this town is located 90° west of Greenwich, meaning a time difference of six hours, we can read of the midnight position (0h) on April 5. We then find in the 90° circle the MC of the catastrophe configuration directly on the axis Mars-Pluto. This configuration in turn coincides with the victim's MC in his cosmogram at the midpoint Sun/Uranus.

Very striking to the eye in **Dr. Luther King**'s cosmogram (Fig. 9) is the opposition of Mars to Saturn. Both factors can be found in the upper right in the 90° circle. **Adolf Hitler** had a similar constellation. At the time of his demise, Mars in progression reached the square to Saturn. Mars-Saturn is a well-known death configuration. Calculating in this case the progressive Mars according to the key 1 day = 1 year after birth, it is then located in the year 1968, in the 39th year of life, at 25° Gemini in an exact opposition to Saturn r. It must be emphasized time and again that significant events in life may be determined by the directions, but they are triggered by the corresponding transits. (In this connection please refer to the books on directions and life diagrams.)

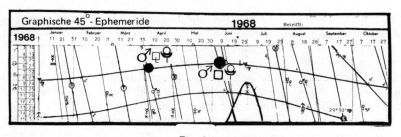

Fig. 8

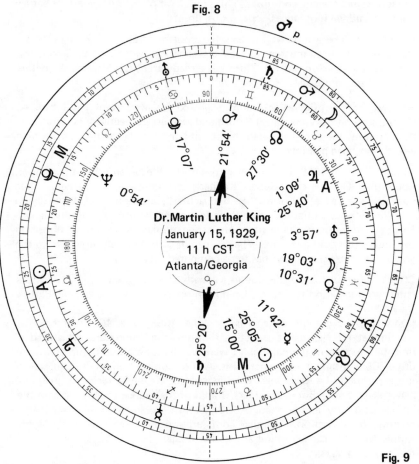

Fig. 9

23

One other decisive configuration contained in the cosmogram is that of Pluto at Midheaven, opposite to Neptune at Sun/Uranus and Uranus/AS. In this context, Pluto = MC means that the native can attain recognition and power and that he sees in his position a kind of mission in life. Neptune opposite can undermine this position and can lead to great disappointments. The CSI gives us the following statements on these positions at Sun/Uranus and Uranus/AS: radical reformer (as a black leader), tragic experience, sudden events and severe shock, the desire to overcome poor conditions and difficult situations, excitement and upset. This configuration was triggered by Saturn points to sudden hindrances, separations, upsets.

Let us now take a look at the Graphic Ephemeris in Fig. 12. Here we see transiting Saturn at the time of the assassination over MC and Saturn (1), triggered by the Sun. At (2), Pluto has already transited Mars weeks before (use of force, murder).

However, this configuration is not triggered by Mars until April 5th. At (3) Mercury and Uranus transit Saturn and Mercury respectively (seperation). If, therefore, the annual diagram had been consulted beforehand, a warning would have been possible.

Around June 5, 1968, Mars again transited the Plutonian orbit, this time in opposition. On this day, **Robert Kennedy** was murdered by **Sirhan**. In the June 1968 issue of "Kosmischer Beobachter", attention was again drawn to: "MA-90-PL, initiating another period of catastrophes and acts of violence." And a repeat of the situation: at the moment of the crime, transiting MC enters this configuartion. (The MC can of course not be derived from the graphic ephemeris, it always has to be computed separately.)

Critical directions are again due in Kennedy's cosmogram (Fig. 10). MC s enters an opposition to Saturn, Uranus an opposition to Uranus, and Pluto s square Sun.

Consulting the graphic ephemeris for June, 1968, (Fig. 12, on the right), we find at (1) Neptune t aspecting Neptune r, a semisquare, which is detrimental in that in the natal chart we have Neptune = Sun/Saturn (with an orb of $1.5°$), meaning a physical crisis. At (2), Jupiter transits the Sun, which in fact should be favorable. Shortly before, **Kennedy** received great applause at a meeting. But Sun at Mars/Uranus in the radix can also indicate the danger of injury and mishap. At (3), Saturn crosses over the Ascendant, pointing to separation. A similar configuration as in the case of **Martin Luther King** can be found at (4): Pluto again transits Mars, triggered by the transiting Mars.

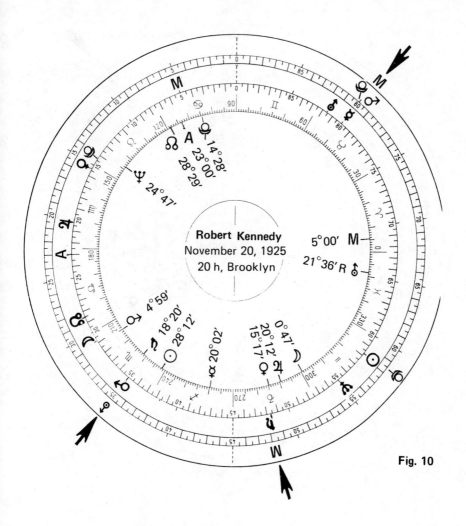

Robert Kennedy
November 20, 1925
20 h, Brooklyn

Fig. 10

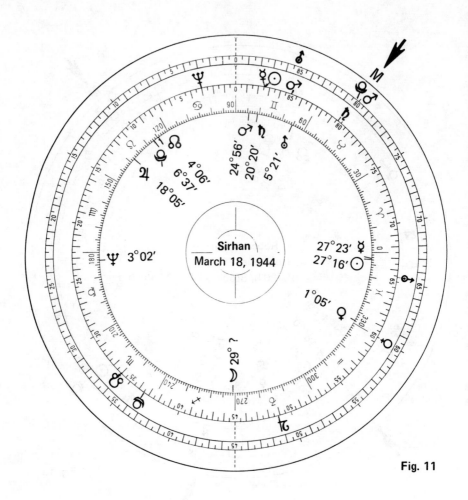

Fig. 11

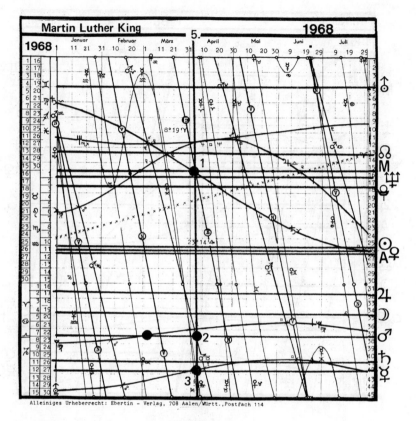

Fig. 12

We might also take a look at the cosmogram of the murderer, **Sirhan** (Fig. 11). In this case, however, we do not have the hour of birth, but with the graphic ephemeris many configurations can be read, even without the MC and AS, especially due to the fact that we do not work with any system of houses, which can be misleading; instead we are only concerned with the actual stellar configurations as they exist.

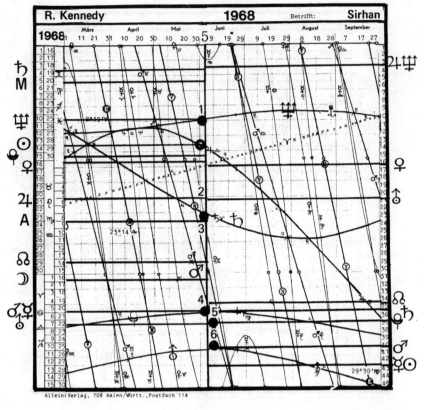

Fig. 12a

At the same place where **Kennedy**'s Mercury and Mars are located we see Saturn and, close by, Pluto, triggered by transiting Pluto and Mars (5). The use of force can also be read from Uranus over Mars (6).

We must admit on going through these examples that they are by no means mere coincidences. In fact, similar configurations, as can always be clearly read from the graphic ephemeris, will always play their role in assassinations. In using **John F. Kennedy**'s cosmogram as yet another example, we could point out the similar Mars-Pluto configurations.

28

DE GAULLE IN THE FACE OF HIS DEFEAT.

General **De Gaulle,** who always called himself the liberator of France, was fully convinced that only he could properly guide the people and bring them good. In the final years, however, unrest and discontent increased. We notice in the natal chart that the positive and negative configurations are in constant equilibrium. Let us observe Pluto and its aspects. Many persons of **De Gaulle's** own age have the conjunction with Neptune, and there is nothing especially characteristic here about it.

Pluto is located at Sun/Moon's Node (desire to compel others, seeking to influence the masses, sharing a common and mass fate) = Mercury/Node (desire for spiritual and mental supremacy over others) = Sun/Saturn (inhibitions in development, serious handicaps) = Saturn/Node (sacrificing oneself for others, suffering because of others, common suffering) = Moon/Mars (onesidedness, fanaticism) = Moon/Jupiter (desire for popularity, attainment of the respect and good thoughts of many). If we transfer these interpretations, which have been quoted almost verbatim from the CSI, to the person of the general and statesman, we will find complete agreement with the life of **De Gaulle.**

When both positive and negative configurations are contained in such a structural picture, as a rule the favorable configurations are triggered by favorable transits and the negative ones by negative transits. In the year 1968 (Fig. 14) we recognize two crises: The Saturn transits over the complex of Neptune — AS — Pluto. France was shaken by revolt, 500,000 Frenchmen were on strike, and **De Gaulle** was compelled to make an unscheduled return from a trip, on May 24 he threatened to resign, on May 25 there was barricade fighting in Paris, and further strikes broke out — all of this generally alluded to as the "hubbub in Paris". There were even posters being carried stating: "Hang **De Gaulle!**". At the end of June, as Jupiter transited the position line of Mercury, the absolute majority cast a favorable vote for **De Gaulle.** We can also see Pluto approaching Jupiter — for the second time — and **De Gaulle** was thus able to retain power.

In November, France was confronted with a finance and currency crisis. November 21 was the so-called "Black Saturday" in Paris. However, the franc was not devaluated after all, due to West German support.

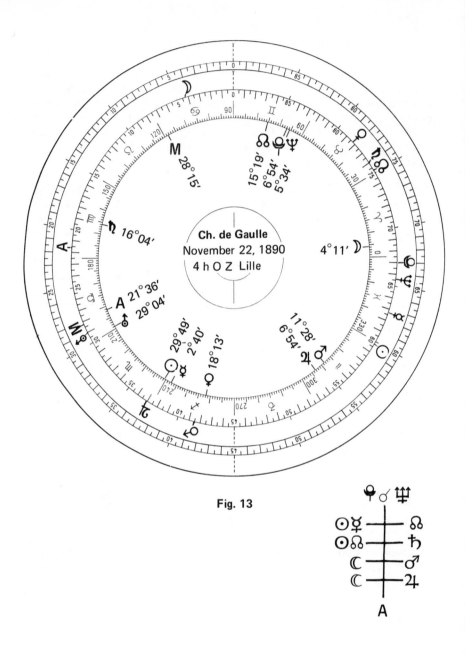

Fig. 13

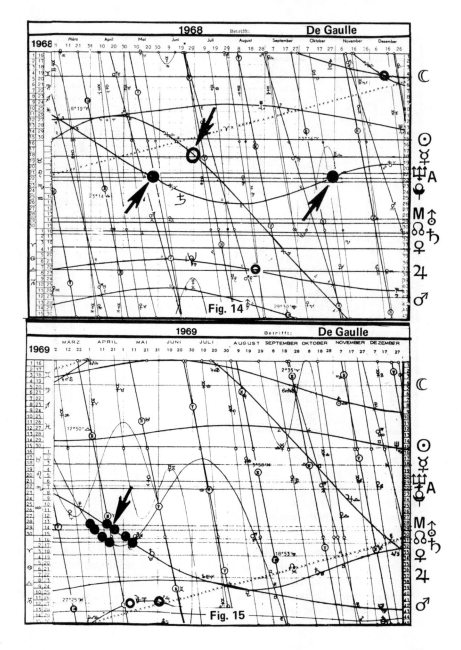

Fig. 14

Fig. 15

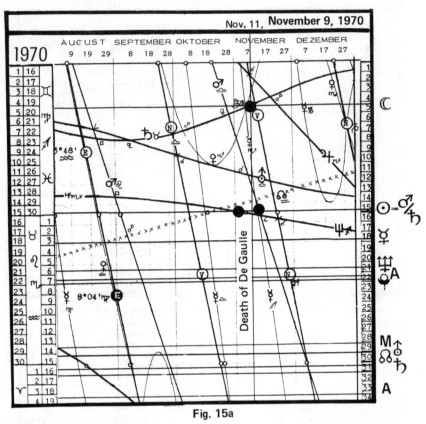

Fig. 15a

In the yearbook for 1969, which came out in the fall of 1968, I stated, among other things: "A severe and vital crisis is possible in April (1969), when Mars and Saturn transit Medium coeli, Uranus and Saturn. Of possible aid to him could be Jupiter over Mars in his attempt to overcome this crisis; nevertheless, he will remain without any chances and will steadily lose his prestige . . . "

De Gaulle threatened to resign on April 10, he demanded a plesbiscite, with the result that with a total voting of 80%, 52% voted in **De Gaulle's** disfavor. On April 28, **Poher**, the president of the senate, became preliminary head of the government. Corresponding to **De Gaulle's** defeat was the positioning of the Saturn transit and Mars in perigee in the same place.

De Gaulle died on November 9, 1970. Here, too, it is very easy to find the corresponding positions in the graphic ephemeris. Saturn is crossing over the Moon, which in this case can be taken to mean separation from the people. Of significance is, however, the transit of Neptune over the Sun, which in the radix is at the midpoint of Mars and Saturn, the so—called death axis. Because of this configuration, the imminence of death is unmistakable.

Let us now take a look at the directions. We find Saturn p at $15°$ 29 Virgo in a square to the Node at $15°$ 19 Gemini. This indicates separation (Saturn) from the community (Moon's Node). Pluto, advanced by measure of the solar arc to $28°$ 14 Leo, is located here in an exact square to the "death axis" Mars/Saturn at $28°$ 46 Scorpio. Using a small orb, we can find further critical directions, for instance, Uranus at $20°$ 24 Sagittarius in a sesquiquadrate to Neptune, and Saturn, at $7°$ 24 Sagittarius, has already gone through the opposition to Pluto.

This clearly demonstrates how prognostications can be made using only the graphic ephemerides. I have in my portfolio the graphic ephemerides of some 150 politicians. I need about one to two hours to look through these each month in order to map out the trends. No other working method has till now rendered such a quick survey possible.

SETTING UP AN ELECTION FORECAST

It is not easy at all to make a correct election forecast weeks or even months beforehand, especially when a configuration such as Jupiter semisquare Neptune, which is particularly evocative of incorrect prognostication, is due. Of prime importance is that the prognosticator preclude from the onset his or others' "wishful thinking" from his investigation; he must take care to evaluate the configurations objectively. Another prerequisite is the comparison with a larger number of persons. A cursory and off—hand investigation can easily result in a false prognostication.

Our investigation is concerned with the West German election in September of 1969. In my monthly surveys I often noticed Pluto approaching Jupiter in the fall of 1969 in the cases of both **Franz Joseph Strauss** and **Karl Schiller.** I concluded from this — especially due to the fact that the time set for the election was not known as yet — that is was entirely possible for these two ministers (each a member of the two traditionally opposing parties, CSU and SPD, resp.) to continue working together in future, but this only in the event of a grand coalition between CDU/CSU and SPD.

After the time of election had been set, I made a general survey of the politicians involved in order to orientate myself for the 21st Work Congress. I found the following contrast: In August, the orbits of Saturn and Pluto in the case of **Schiller** struck Saturn, with **Strauss** the MC. This could only lead to the conclusion that any kind of cooperation between the two ministers appeared to be impossible and that in fact the differences would widen. It is obvious that **Strauss'** success configuration comes about the beginning of September (Fig. 21) when he did indeed receive a great deal of attention and response due to his speeches. Subsequently, however, Saturn approaches MC (difficulties, failure), and, above, Uranus transits Pluto (upset, tension), and this involved unpleasant clashes with the young revolutionists. At the time of the election, Neptune transits Mars (paralysis, disappointment, illness), and Jupiter transits Saturn (vexation, trouble). This means, therefore, that prospects at the time of election were very poor.

Things looked completely different in **Schiller's** case, who in fact always showed confidence. The critical situation in August is expressed here, too, in the transits of Saturn and Pluto over Saturn. At this point, however, Pluto approaches the complex of Node, Jupiter and Pluto, that is, the success configuration in this particular radix. The due date lies somewhere between the end of September and the middle of October. At the same time, Jupiter transits Mars, and in contrast, it transits Saturn in the case of **Strauss.** It could,

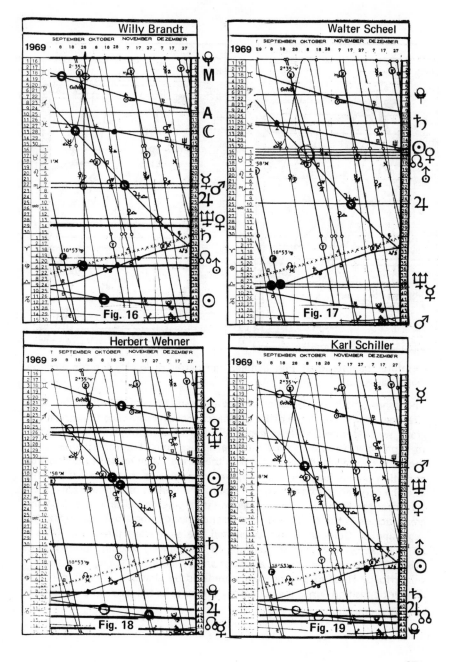

Fig. 16 — Willy Brandt

Fig. 17 — Walter Scheel

Fig. 18 — Herbert Wehner

Fig. 19 — Karl Schiller

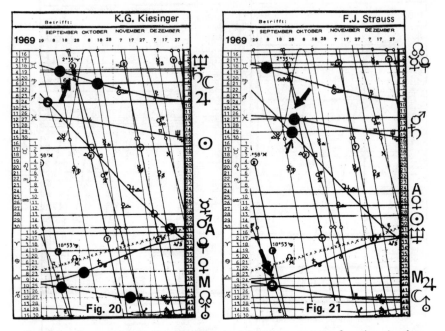

Fig. 20 — K.G. Kiesinger

Fig. 21 — F.J. Strauss

therefore, be presumed that **Schiller** had better prospects for the election than **Strauss** did.

The more important question, however, was that of whether Dr. **Kurt Kiesinger** would retain the office of Chancellor. On examining the annual diagram, we find immediately evident the many black dots, i.e. negative points. In September, Uranus first transits the "illness axis" Saturn/Neptune. Since the same constellation was also due in the spring, when he had to undergo an operation on his jaw, there was reason for supposing that he could become ill or be exposed to extra stress and strain. The transits of Sun, Mars and Mercury over the Moon around the election date gave no indication at all of any great success in the offing. Mars over Jupiter was to bring about decisions at the beginning of October. I also calculated the significant directions: Mars p (3° 23 Cancer) conjunction Neptune (3° 17 Cancer) sesquiquadrate Saturn (18° 39 Aquarius) pointed to a lack of energy, failures, "paralysed activity", vain efforts. These directions were stimulated by Uranus t. We may consider Jupiter opposition Sun in the middle of October to be too weak to produce any notable momentum.

36

If therefore, the party leaders, **Kiesinger** and **Strauss**, together had no good prospects at all, then there must be favorable configurations present for those of the opposing party, the SPD.

I had noted many years before that in the case of **Willy Brandt** Jupiter p conjunction Uranus would become due around 1969, meaning advancement for him at this time. We see in the annual diagram Pluto approaching the Sun. This configuration becomes due in October and indicates power of assertion and a striving for power. We do not know **Willy Brandt's** exact time of birth, but the solar position should be fairly correct. The MC could shift by about 1°, in which case transits of Uranus, Sun, Mars over the MC would have been due on the day of election. Jupiter over Moon at the end of the month led to an increase in his popularity, which consequentially meant more votes. After the middle of October, Saturn over Uranus could mean the sudden arise of problems, and Neptune over Moon could dampen the public esteem. It looks like the election might not go so smoothly after all. At the beginning of November, the success complex Mars—Mercury—Jupiter is transited by Jupiter.

Brandt's success is very strongly dependent on his "party strategist", **Herbert Wehner**. In his annual diagram, we see Pluto approaching Jupiter, thus meaning the presence of an unusual success configuration. Nonetheless, Saturn over Pluto and Jupiter over Neptune can only be termed negative. In October, Jupiter over Sun and Mars are counted as positive.

Walter Scheel's annual diagram was of particular interest. Up to the end of September, it is negative in tone due to Saturn and Pluto over Neptune, Neptune over Saturn, and Jupiter over Saturn. But at the beginning of October, Jupiter transits the complex of Sun, Venus, Uranus, Node. Now taking a look at the diagrams of **Brandt** and **Wehner**, we find they have this Jupiter configuration in common, this making a joint success likely. What one could hardly foresee was the odd way in which this success was to come about.

At the 21st Work Congress I therefore presented in manuscript form the following prognostication: Jupiter semisquare Neptune indicates incorrect forecasts at this time. One can see from the axis Jupiter/Neptune = Saturn/Node that there can be great difficulties in the way of partners coming to terms, or that the one partner will feel disappointed, injured, or cheated by the other. The lunar eclipse together with Mars and Uranus indicates incidents, demonstrations, unrest (316 injured during the election campaign, of these 124 were civilians and 192 policemen). These configurations now have to be correlated with the cosmograms of the politicians involved. At the time of election, the Incumbent Chancellor, **Kurt Kiesinger,** was most likely not in the best of health, and his situation can be considered only in a slightly favorable light. The direction of Mars to Neptune can mean at the very least a severe disappointment or susceptibility to disease.

F.J. Strauss will show a great deal of pre-election activity. Neptune over Mars and Jupiter over Saturn at the end of September could lead to disappointment. With von **Hassel, Benda, Katzer,** and **Schröder,** other prominent members of the Union, there are ample negative influences present, lending foundation to the presumption that the CDU/CSU will not achieve their goal.

On the FDP side, **Walter Scheel** will have many difficulties to deal with before the election, but successes after election day are not unlikely.

This all more or less substantiates the election forecast. For those not familiar with the actual election results: The CDU/CSU and the SPD both achieved approximately the same number of votes,and the FDP in effect lost the election. However, talks between the SPD and the FDP had taken place previous to the election which made it possible for **Scheel** to join up with **Brandt** immediately, and a new coalition was formed. **Willy Brandt** became the new Chancellor.

There are many other examples we can take from politics where prognostications based on the graphic ephemerides have been made and substantiated. In order, however, to give this book greater variety and scope, the following pages will present the successes and failures of individual persons and will then go on to various diseases and other aspects of life.

THE FIVE-MILLION POUND POST ROBBERY

On August 8, 1963 a British postal train was held-up and robbed. The robbers' take amounted to 5 million pounds sterling. One of the leaders of the band was **Ronald Biggs**. According to the information given by various journalists and commentators, he was born on August 8, 1930.

The hour of birth is not known, but one of the great merits of the graphic ephemerides is that a prognostication is possible even without knowledge of the birth-time, if one knows enough about the person in question and his circumstances.

One would expect to find here certain correspondences to Mars, Pluto (violence), to Jupiter (successful enterprise), and to Saturn (separation, escape, travel). This is indeed the case. However, there are not many hints to be found among the traditional aspects. Clearer indications can be had in the cosmogram from the midpoint combinations in the $90°$ circle, for instance, Mars = Sun/Pluto: Extraordinary ambition, overstrain, ruthlessness.

Before making a prognostication on the basis of the graphic ephemeris, it is always a good idea to take a close look at the natal chart and to note the most important structural elements. Hence, alongside the cosmogram we may also make use of a listing of the various midpoint relationships. The following are the most predominent configurations:

PL = ME/NE: Unusual acts, placing great demands on one's nervous energy, an actor.

SO = MA/UR: Capability of sudden increase in physical energy, person capable of quick action.

UR= SO/MA: Precipitancy, impulsive action, exceeding the limits of one's energies — in criminal cases: arrest.

UR= JU/PL: Fanatical striving for reform, quick grasp of any situation — successful organization.

These are the configurations which have to be substantiated by the events. At the time of the robbery, the solar arc was $31°$ 50. Adding this to Mars, we get Mars s = $18°$ 54 Cancer, almost a conjunction with Pluto. Together with Pluto = Mercury/Neptune this results in: Thinking directed towards one's goal, rich imagination (ingenuity), the realization of plans, acting on consideration and from experience.

Mercury + Solar arc = $38°$ 51 = $8°$ 51 Libra, i.e. square Jupiter = Venus/Pluto = Sun/Neptune: Success, unusual good luck, success without any special effort.

Sun + solar arc = 17° 52 Libra − 90 − Mars 17° 04 Gemini = Sun/Pluto = Mercury/Venus: Overcoming difficulties and danger (CSI 218) through unusual energy and effort. On transcribing the positions from the natal chart to the Graphic Ephemeris for 1963, we immediately notice one very particular configuration. This is the aspect of Jupiter and Uranus which coincides with the natal Pluto. One might object that this configuration is due for a great number of persons having Pluto in this position. But in this case, Pluto is located in the natal chart at the midpoint Mercury/Neptune, as ascertained previously, and which points to unusual acts, high demands made on nervous energy, and acting talent. This configuration, therefore, is given individual coloring through Mercury/Neptune. In addition, the Moon's Node comes to meet this configuration in the Graphic Ephemeris, the Node in combination with Jupiter and Uranus, thus indicating joint, sudden good luck or some special success. If **Biggs'** birth-time were known, one could certainly apply some personal points as well. One unfavorable aspect is that in the lower part of the ephemeris Neptune transits Venus at the end of August, which can be considered an undermining or denial of love-life, he did indeed become separated from his wife due to his imprisonment. In addition a series of critical Mars aspects over Uranus, Neptune, Pluto appears from the middle of August onward, and this is, therefore, probably the time at which he was arrested.

For precise investigations we use the Graphic 45° −Midpoint Ephemeris, in which, as the name states, the current midpoints are also entered. The following figure   presents a section of this Ephemeris for July and August, 1963. We notice here that the midpoint Jupiter/Pluto transits the solar position at the beginning of August, indicating sudden good luck, i.e. in combination with the solar position. However, as we can see just below, the midpoint Saturn/Neptune is approaching the Sun, and this tends to set a limit to the good luck.

The robber succeeded in escaping after spending two years in prison and since has been roaming around the world from place to place. His money brought **Biggs** no luck after all, as he has used every last penny of it and has had to go back to a job. The story of his life has been published many times over in newspapers and magazines, so that is not necessary to go in to it here.

This example demonstrates how success in many fields of enterprise can be read from the Graphic Ephemeris. It has also been shown that on this basis any number of persons can be observed and their possible successes or failures mapped for the future. If, for example, there is knowledge of a particular crime being planned, one could under circumstances set the date for its possible execution, and it is also possible to determine when a certain criminal has poor constellations due, in which case there might be an increased chance at that time to capture him.

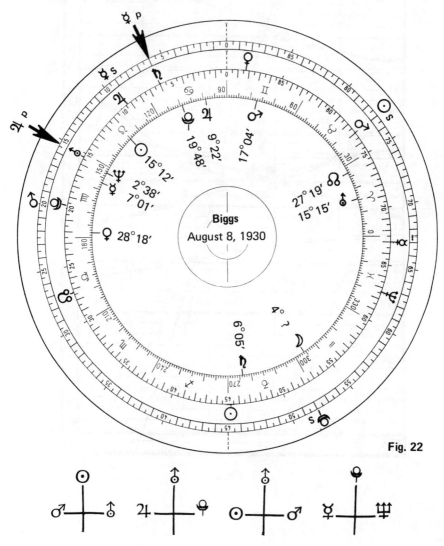

Fig. 22

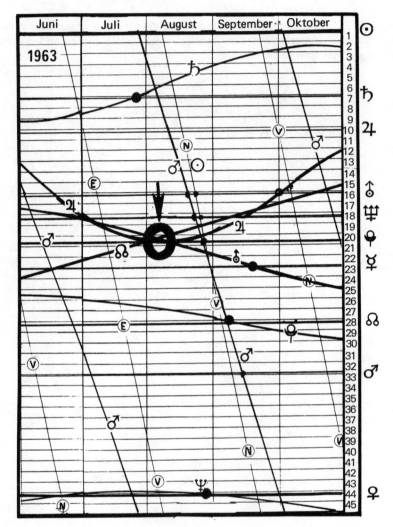

Fig. 23

42

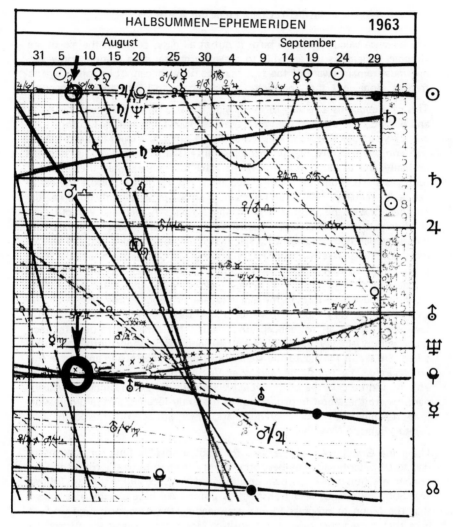

Fig. 24

THE CALCULATION OF A BIRTH

The advance calculation of a birth is not at all easy, but with the aid of the Graphic Ephemeris we are able to survey a greater span of time. However, one must remain aware of the fact that the problem cannot be solved by the transits alone, but that the directions also have to be taken into account.

This case concerns a female birth on May 6, 1923, at 4h 55m (a.m.) at 51°N and 6°46 E. The mother, whom we shall call **Inge Lehmann**, or I.L. for short, was 27 years old when she married and gave birth to a child two years later, but who due to a blood-group incompatibility (rhesus factor) did not develop normally and is today still in a home. The father died when the child was four years old. The mother hesitated until her 38th year before she could decide to remarry. Her second husband was not in particularly good health, but nevertheless he wanted a child and stated: "A marriage without any children just isn't a marriage." His wife was above all afraid of complications such as which had occurred with her first child, and besides that she was already somewhat late in years for a pregnancy. On closely examining the natal chart, I noticed that in the year 1965/66 progressive Mars transits Venus. On the date of birth in 1966 Mars pr was located at 11° 59 Cancer, and accordingly it must have formed the exact square to Venus in the year 1965. As we know, this very aspect of Venus and Mars is decisive for all matters of love and, above all, for conception and birth. No time was to be lost, since she was now already past the age of 40, and every opportunity had to be taken. We see in the figure the stellar positions in progression entered in the outer circle. The transit of Mars over Venus, top left, is very striking (Fig. 25). In addition, in the outer circle we find Jupiter approaching the Ascendant, where the Moon in progression is presently located. Sun in progression is approaching the midpoint Venus/Mars, which lies opposite the complex of Jupiter, Sun and Neptune.

Using the Graphic 45°—Ephemeris for 1965 a possible time for conception had to be determined. The best opportunity seemed to be the transit in September of Jupiter over its own position and the Sun, and in the days following, Sun and Venus also transit these points. We have already ascertained that the Moon in progression was approaching the Ascendant, and we find here that during this time, the transiting Moon, too, crosses the Ascendant and Jupiter together with Sun. It therefore would be possible that the Moon in progression could be triggered during this transit by the transiting Moon. There were other transits due at this time as well, such as the transits of Sun and Venus over Moon, Mars, and Uranus. In September, it was already high time for

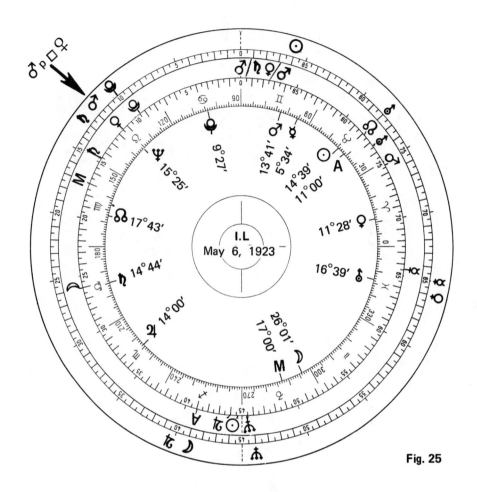

Fig. 25

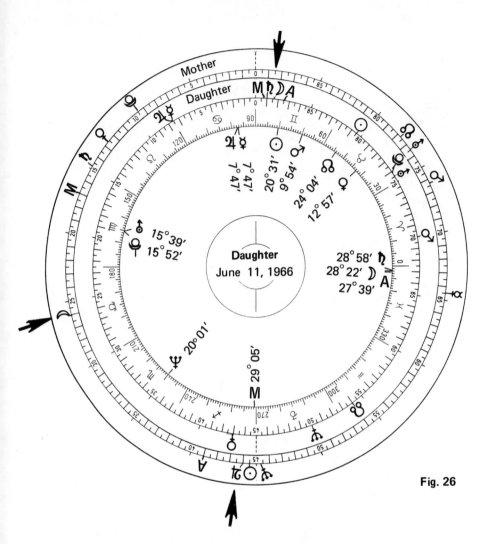

Fig. 26

conception to take place, since the coming months would see the very unfavorable Saturn aspect to the Moon. It was, therefore, recommended that the
time around the beginning of September was best for a conception, and the
couple was advised to be more continent prior to this time, in order to be
better prepared. She did become pregnant, and it was now necessary to calculate the probable date of birth, which should occur around the beginning of

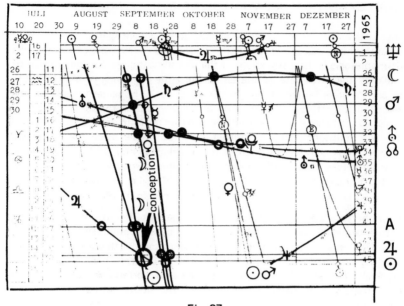

Fig. 27

June 1966. However, Saturn aspected Jupiter and Sun here, yet the configuration of Jupiter and Sun was also triggered about June 11 by Venus and also the transiting Moon. It has been frequently observed that natal Moon and conception Moon coincide. There was this possibility here, and indeed, the birth took place just at this time, on June 11, 1966, at 23h 10m. The parents were overjoyed, and this was reflected by the transit of Jupiter over Pluto and Venus in the weeks subsequent to the birth.

We must also add that the Jupiter-Sun aspect of the mother also aspects the father's Venus. The mother's 90° circle was laid around the circumference of the child's cosmogram, making the various points of contact recognizable, although not as clearly as with the Graphic Ephemeris, since only the 90° aspects can be read and not the 45° aspects as well. At any rate, we can clearly define the mother's complex of Jupiter, Sun, Neptune in contrast to that of the child's Ascendant, Moon, Saturn and MC.

THE CORRECT CALCULATION OF A BIRTH — A WORK PROBLEM

Many births have been correctly calculated in advance. In the 73rd work problem, which was presented in the September 1970 issue of the journal, "Kosmobiologie", the cosmogram of the mother was given for the purpose of calculating the birth-date of the child, born the beginning of March, 1969. The child's grandfather, using the Graphic 45° —Ephemeris, had already chosen the correct day of birth. And it was then put up to the readers of the journal named to see if they were also able to find the right date. Unfortunately, only ten solutions were submitted, and of these, four were correct, since they took the date of birth to be the 9th of March, 1969. Two persons almost succeeded in finding the correct answer, they named March 8. Due to the fact that the child was born on March 9 at 0h 50m, i.e. shortly after midnight, this answer can also be counted as right. Only four solutions were false.

The mother was born on December 1, 1945, at 22h 30m in Bremen (Fig. 28). The solar arc is 23° 38. We find the following configurations in the outer 90° circle: Uranus s —135— Venus s, a conception and birth constellation very frequently observed. Not only Jupiter s—180—MC means personal happiness or special success; MC at Venus/Mars can also correspond to a felicitous birth. Progressive Venus is semisquare to the Moon, which among other things can also apply to expectant mothers. At the same time, Pluto s —45— Jupiter is at Venus/Uranus, pointing to a successful delivery.

It is known that the birth is supposed to take place at the beginning of March, 1969. Looking at the Graphic 45°- Ephemeris in Fig. 28a, we see the direction Pluto s = Jupiter = Venus/Uranus triggered by Mars t. on the 9th. Mercury t crosses Venus, Venus t crosses the Sun as well as Saturn. The Sun transits Mars and thereby triggers the direction Venus s—135—Mars.

This example clearly illustrates the interplay of directions and transits and how they should be combined.

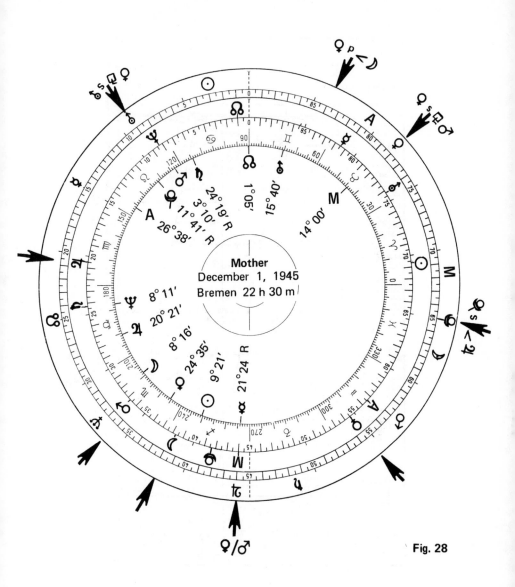

Fig. 28

49

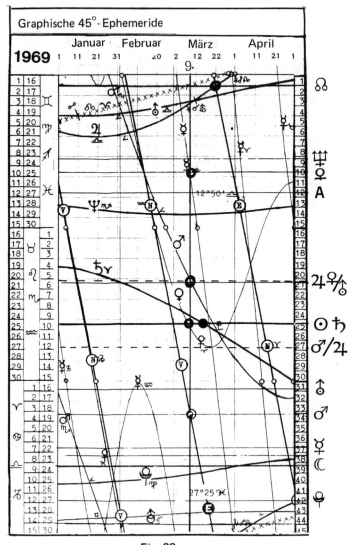

Fig. 28a

THE DANGER OF FALSE PROGNOSTICATIONS

By no means should one assume that everything can be read and mapped by means of the Graphic Ephemerides. The importance of the directions and the fact of the transits acting more or less as triggering elements will be substantiated time and again. Returning to the example given in Fig. 26, we will remember that the first husband died four years after the birth of his child. In this same case, death recurs likewise in a child's fourth year, the death of the mother.

The beginning of August, 1970 I received the news the Mrs. I L. had suffered a severe stroke on Sunday, July 26, 1970, at 16h 45m, and was in a very critical condition. I was asked to examine the case and frankly state what I thought the prospects were. The Graphic Ephemeris (Fig.29) makes it evident that around July 26 first Mars and then Sun and Venus transit Uranus, which most certainly can allude to a stroke. Besides this, Pluto is approaching the Ascendant, but which does not necessarily have to be considered especially critical. Of significance, however, is the transit of Neptune over Saturn and that this transit is repeated in the fall of the year. This gives an idea of the severity of the attack.

We see in the cosmogram of Mrs. I.L. that at the time of the child's birth progressive Mars aspected Venus, but in the years following had been approaching Saturn. Experience has shown that an aspect of Mars and Saturn always makes an appearance in times of death and hence can mean vital danger.

This made me recognize the gravity of the situation, and I did not quite know what I was to tell the husband. It was impossible to say that her death could possibly be expected within the next few days; after all, it might have been possible for her to overcome the crisis. Therefore, I wrote to him saying that the configuration Mars p square Saturn could be considered a death configuration, but that there was hope of recovery in the event of the favorable Jupiter configurations over Mars, Uranus and Moon's Node turning up in the near future. Also to be taken into account was the transit at the end of October of Jupiter together with Pluto over Jupiter and Sun, and that, by then perhaps, a recovery could be achieved.

However, in this case, Jupiter and Sun are by no means favorably positioned because of their aspects to Neptune, located in the 360° circle exactly on the midpoint of Sun and Jupiter. In addition, the Sun and Jupiter are at the midpoint of Mars and Saturn, which is in itself implicative of death. It now depended on how the configuration on August 10 would resolve when Mars

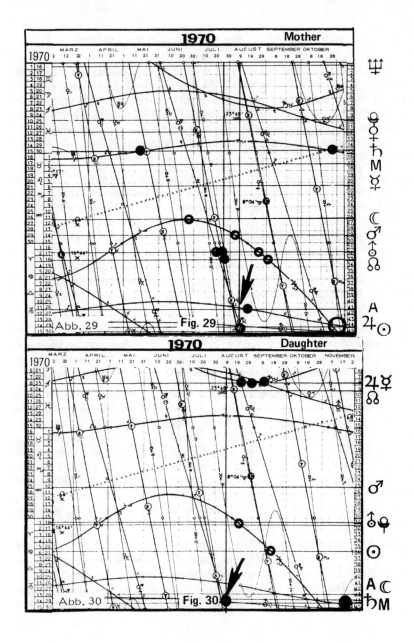

1970   Mother

Abb. 29   Fig. 29

1970   Daughter

Abb. 30   Fig. 30

transited Sun and Jupiter and at the same time the midpoint Mars/Saturn. It was negative, since I.L.'s death came on August 10.

This example should serve as a warning against incautious prognostication, for, as we can see, not everything is to be read from the configurations alone.

We discover in the annual diagram of the little daughter (Fig.30) that transiting Mars crosses the complex of Moon, Saturn and MC. This is the decisive point of contact, which was already ascertained at the birth of the child. In addition, Saturn and MC were in close conjunction at birth, and at the age of four, progressive Saturn had just transited the MC.

THE EVOLUTION OF THE CONCEPTION COSMOGRAM

The Viennese physician, **Heinz Fidelsberger,** M.D., head of the Viennese Astrological Society, carried out an experiment concerning cosmic twins. He discovered that on April 25, 1947, in a gynaecological clinic in Vienna, birth was given to two boys at the very same time by women lying in beds right next to each other in the same maternity ward. Both boys, therefore, had the same cosmic natal chart in common. In addition, it was determined that both boys had the same weight and length at birth; in the course of time, however, differences did develop. This experiment was described in detail in the January 1968 issue of the journal, "Kosmobiologie".

Of interest for the purpose of our investigation are the birth dates of the parents in relation to birth and conception. The two natives are called here **Ernst** and **Ferdinand,** or E. and F. respectively. Accordingly, F.M. means **Ferdinand's** mother and F.F. **Ferdinand's** father, and of course, **E.M. Ernst's** mother and **E.F. Ernst's** father. The parents' hours of birth are unknown to us, yet we will still be able to bring evidence of many coinciding configurations. The natal chart of the two natives is given in Fig. 35. Fig. 36 results from the transcription of the natal positions of the two mothers in the Graphic Ephemeris for the year 1947. Here, F.M.'s position lines are continuous and those of E.M. are dotted. Our first discovery is that similar configurations are present with both F.M. and E.M., e.g. in the first case Jupiter together with Mars are to be found in almost the same position as Jupiter and Venus in the second case. We may, therefore, assume that these configurations had some special influence on the births. This is in fact the case, since Venus transited this common point on April 25. Furthermore, we find Venus F.M. and Sun E.M. coinciding. This configuration was jointly triggered by transiting Sun. Finally, we discover the Uranus positions on almost the same spot, and these were jointly stimulated by transiting Venus. We must also make note of the fact there is an age difference of 12 years between the two women and that despite this, there is this concurrence of factors at the time of the births.

What we now need to find are the corresponding configurations at the time of conception. So—called conception horoscopes used to be cast, in which one merely counted the usual 273 days backwards from the time of birth. As a method this is inprecise, since not all births occur according to a set schedule, some take place later than they should and some prematurely. In general, the rule applies that the lunar position at the time of conception and at the time of birth is approximately the same. It is likely that conception came about at the end of July, 1946.

I have calculated the Graphic Ephemeris for July, 1946, and entered the configurations for the two mothers. As a result, the transits of Sun and Venus over the common position lines of Venus F.M. and Sun E.M. become evident. These configurations indicate in particular physical (Sun) love (Venus). Another factor, however, is that the Mars positions of the two husbands are at the same location, and it becomes clear that when Sun and Venus transit woman's Venus and the man's Mars, or the woman's Sun and the man's Mars as well, conception can take place.

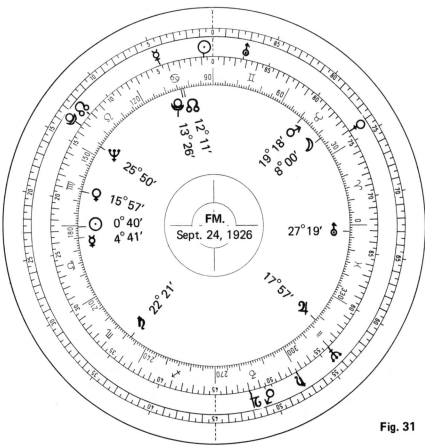

Fig. 31

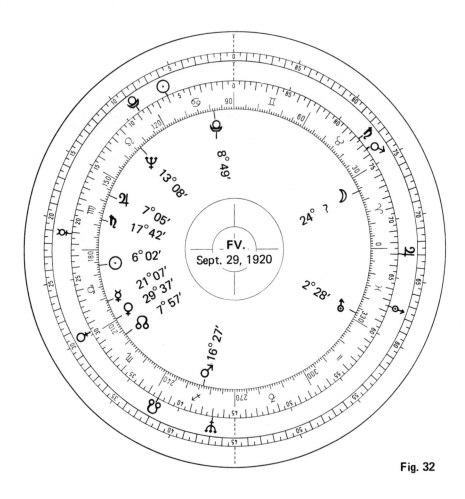

Fig. 32

As far as I know, this sort of investigation has to date never been carried out, and I would like to recommend the treatment of other examples in this manner, it might thus be possible to ascertain the true conception configurations. Although a number of conception configurations are known, it would still be of advantage to have more comprehensive evidence available in order to find out the best times for conception in advance.

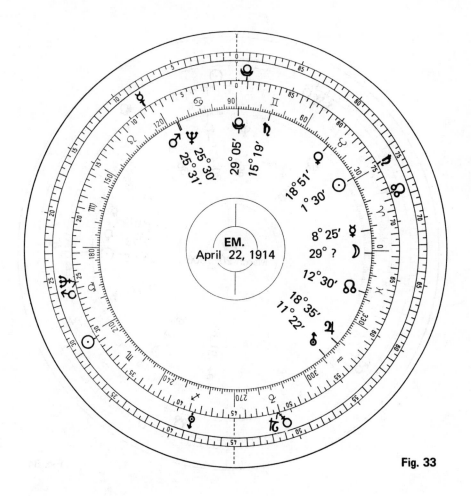

Fig. 33

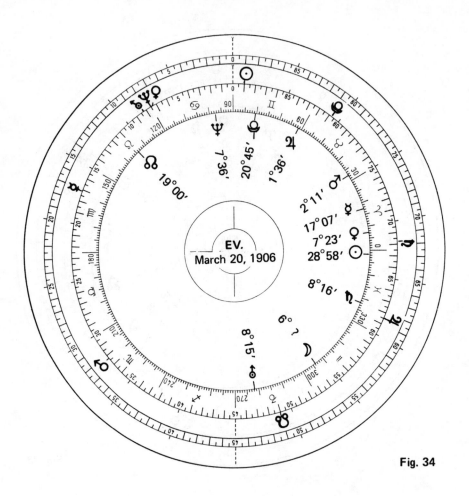

Fig. 34

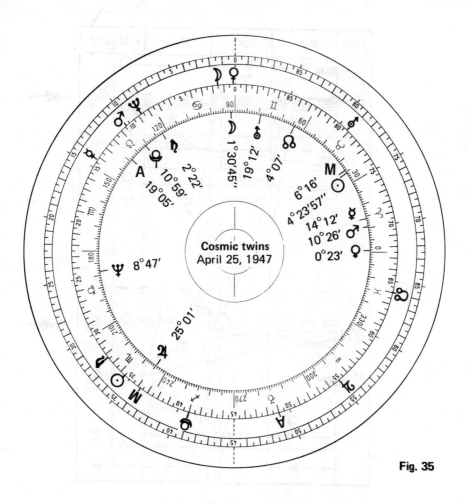

Fig. 35

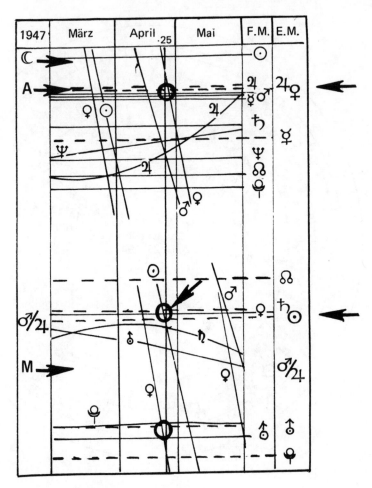

Fig. 36

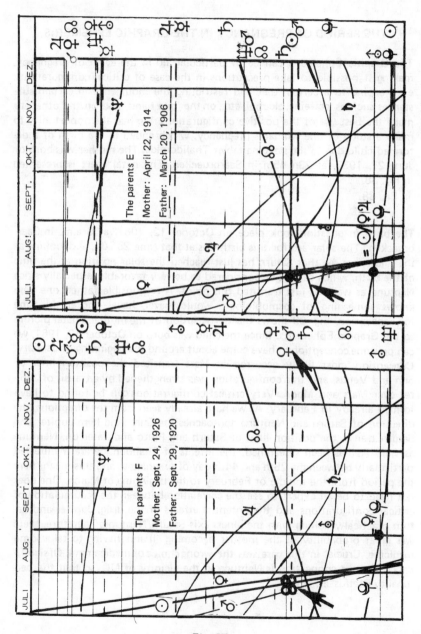

Fig. 37

THE PERIOD OF PREGNANCY IN THE GRAPHIC EPHEMERIS

The Graphic Ephemeris can be of particular aid in the event of pregnancy, making it possible to take precautions in the case of critical configurations, e.g. keeping to a certain diet and restricting the indulgence in certain substances such as caffeine, alcohol, etc., on the one hand, and on the other, to make the best use of the positive configurations. We had the opportunity to make a study of one woman's pregnancy, which ended in the birth of a deformed child due to the sleeping tablet Thalidomide. The mother was born on June 27, 1935, at 23h 45m in Saarbruecken. The natal chart is presented in Fig. 38.
in Fig. 38.

The birth in question took place on October 12, 1961, at 6 a.m. in Saarbruecken. The solar arc for this birth was at that time 25° 04, and looking at the figure, we see that Saturn has just reached the solar position at the time of the birth, which cannot be considered to be very favorable, especially since Neptune as well has just transited this point. A responsible father, one who knows something of cosmobiology, would never have chosen this time for conception. Fig. 39 shows the transcription of the mother's natal picture to the Graphic Ephemeris. Since the child was born on October 12, 1961, we can presume conception to have come about around the beginning of January. Conception most likely occurred as Mars transited the position lines of Sun and Venus, and this configuration was strengthened by a transit of Jupiter over Mars and Moon. Very critical configurations can be found to have formed already in February. As we have already seen from the directions, the direction of Saturn and Neptune approaches the Sun. And here Jupiter and Saturn transit the position lines of Saturn and Pluto and, later on, Neptune as well. As has been researched, the effects of Thalidomide are manifested particularly between the 25th and 44th day of pregnancy, and this means here the period from the middle of February to the beginning of March. One does not need to be an expert to see the correlation between the accumulation of critical configurations and the potential effects of the drug; Jupiter and Saturn practically collide with the illness axis Saturn/Neptune. Therefore, there was great probability of the mother becoming ill and having to take some medicine. Crucial in this case was the wrong choice of medicament. Of significance in this connection is Neptune in the vicinity of MC, so that the personality itself is affected.

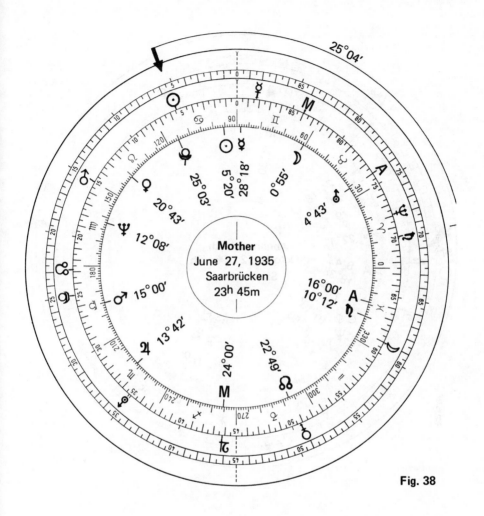

Fig. 38

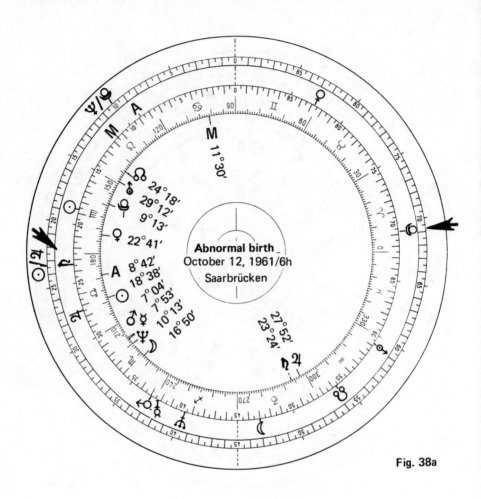

Fig. 38a

Let us now take a look at the last few months previous to the birth. Saturn t and Pluto t approach the critical position lines of Saturn and Pluto. Jupiter t aspects Neptune, and Neptune t aspects MC and Mercury. This is, therefore, much the same configuration as in the spring. The birth took place during New Moon on October 12, and it is also likely that conception took place just before New Moon. I have done research on a number of pregnancies and have always made the discovery that similar factors and symptoms made their appearance, even if they were not of such grave consequence as in the case of Thalidomide users, that led to certain abnormalities.

In parenthesis I might add that in the case of the Thalidomide—children, heliocentric configurations in particular were present, in which significant planets were located at the midpoints of Earth/Saturn. In carrying out such investigations, it is of the greatest importance not to let the expectant mother have a look at the Graphic Ephemerides, to avoid her being unduly influenced. The Graphic Ephemerides are intended only for the information of the father or the physician, so that corresponding measures can be taken in time. Above all, one should not give way to such pronostications which not only would rob the mother of all hope, but would also make any treatment more difficult.

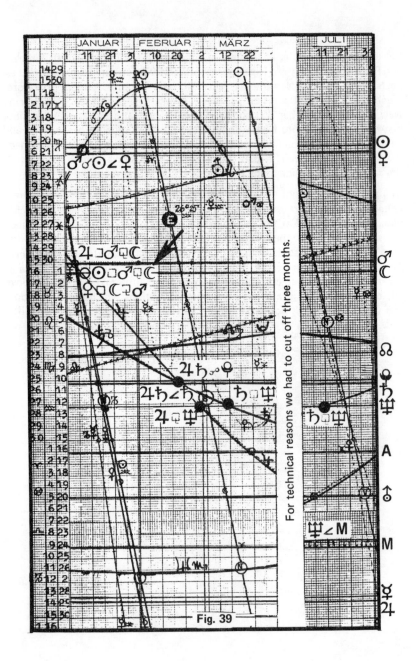

Fig. 39

For technical reasons we had to cut off three months.

66

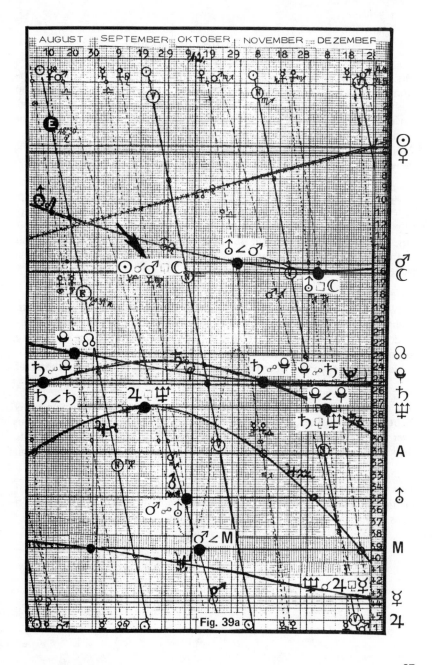

Fig. 39a

ILLNESS DURING PREGNANCY

Mrs. **Herta Schulze** of Berlin sent some time ago the following case: A woman, who was born on February 20, 1934, in Berlin, became pregnant in the year 1966. In August she suffered from an inflammation of the abdominal veins, and apparently had not been given the correct treatment from the start; on August 19, 1966, she was admitted to the hospital, and on October 21 it became necessary to induce birth. She was totally unconscious during delivery. The child was born on October 21 at 22h 20m.

Crucial directions were due for the year 1966: Mars s—45—Sun = Saturn/Neptune = Mars/Saturn, i.e. a very critical illness configuration, Venus s—90—Neptune = Saturn/MC = Moon/MC, also a very grave direction, and MC s—90—Venus, the configuration of birth. But even leaving aside the directions, a crisis in the summer months is immediately evident in the annual diagram, when Neptune t aspects MC and Saturn.

However, there is compensation in the form of some favorable Jupiter transits over Sun, Ascendant, Jupiter, Uranus and Mars; at the time of birth there is Jupiter—135—Mercury. Since conception probably took place in January, we can find here the transits of Jupiter, Venus and Sun over the natal Venus, which would mean the strong physical attraction of one partner to the other.

The delivery took place under complete narcosis, typical of this is Sun t over Neptune, whereas a surgical delivery corresponds to Sun over Mars. Venus over Jupiter indicates the joy of the mother. In the period after the birth difficulties are in evidence due to Saturn and Uranus t combined with Venus.

It is my hope that parents will have learned from this example that a conception should only be considered of when the mother's annual diagram contains a mere minimum of critical configurations.

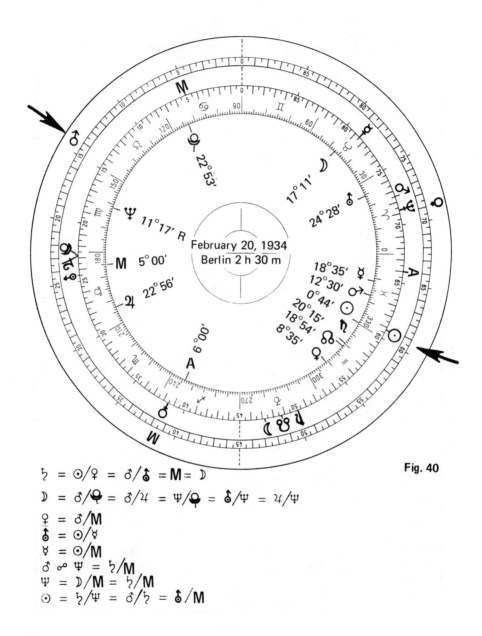

February 20, 1934
Berlin 2 h 30 m

Fig. 40

$\hbar = \odot/\varphi = \delta/\mathbf{\delta} = M = \mathbb{D}$

$\mathbb{D} = \delta/\mathbf{Q} = \delta/\mathbf{2} = \Psi/\mathbf{Q} = \mathbf{\delta}/\Psi = \mathbf{2}/\Psi$

$\varphi = \delta/M$

$\mathbf{\delta} = \odot/\forall$

$\forall = \odot/M$

$\delta \,\infty\, \Psi = \hbar/M$

$\Psi = \mathbb{D}/M = \hbar/M$

$\odot = \hbar/\Psi = \delta/\hbar = \mathbf{\delta}/M$

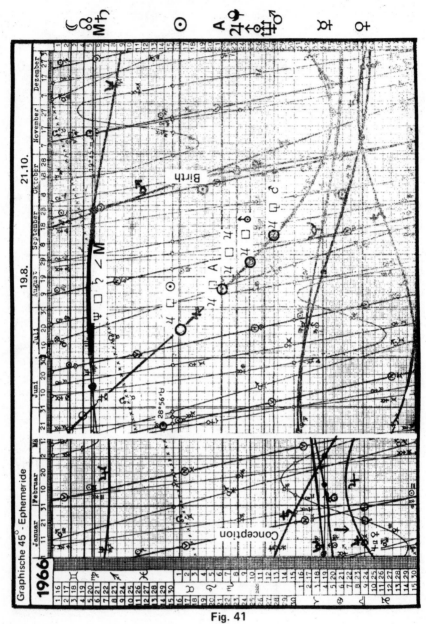

Fig. 41

HOW TO FIND THE BEST DAY FOR A MARRIAGE

It is the desire of every couple in love to be truly happy on the day their marriage takes place. However, this does not always turn out to be the case. I can recall one case where the mother of the bride died just a few days before the day of the wedding. Since all the preparations had been completed and a number of relations were to come from far away, a postponement of the wedding was no longer possible, and grief overshadowed any joy one may have felt. Illness and mishap can also play a role, in making a postponement necessary. Therefore, it is correct to take the precaution of looking through the annual diagrams of the individuals involved and to set the date for the wedding accordingly.

We have selected one example from our archives, the "fairy tale wedding" of Crown Princess **Margarete** of Danemark and Prince **Hendrik.** We do not know whether this wedding had been calculated cosmobiologically, but one thing is sure, the bride gave the impression of being very happy. And this indeed corresponds to the configurations due.

The outer 90° circle of the Princess contains the solar arc directions due (Fig. 42), among these, Jupiter s strikes the Moon, pointing to a happy (Jupiter) woman (Moon), and located opposite are Venus and Mars s, which, in combination with Moon and Jupiter, can mean marital felicity.

Uranus s at MC opposite Pluto is primarily indicative of a sudden turn (Uranus) in personal (MC) fate (Pluto). Less favorable is Neptune s over Sun, giving rise to certain disappointments.

In the contact cosmogram, Fig. 43, in the center of which we show a picture of the wedding couple, we can see on the righthand side at (1) Mars m (m=male, f =female) aspected with Venus f and opposite Jupiter and Sun f. This is the configuration which is mainly the foundation of a strong physical attraction. As we will remember from the directions, Venus, Mars f were triggered by Jupiter s. At (2), Moon m and MC f are harmoniously combined, but Saturn f is located opposite (4). Pluto m = AS, Jupiter f at (3) can be considered a strong aspect.

In looking at Princess **Margarete's** annual diagram (Fig.44) we will find she really has chosen the right day for the wedding. Jupiter and Pluto meet, signifying: great (Pluto) happiness (Jupiter) in combination with the MC, applying to one's own self. However, Saturn is also involved, forming a semisquare to Saturn in the radix. Nevertheless, Saturn does not necessarily have to be negative, but rather, in this case, it merely underlines the earnestness of the

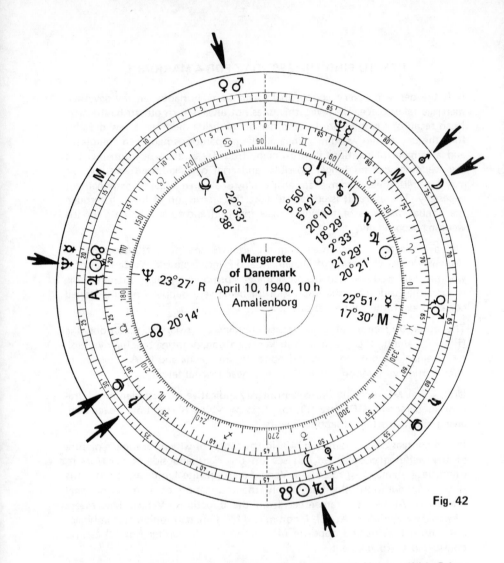

Margarete of Danemark
April 10, 1940, 10 h
Amalienborg

Ψ 23°27' R

℞ 20°14'

♀♂

22°33'
0°38'

5°50'
5°42'
20°10'
18°29'
2°33'
21°29'
20°21'

22°51' ☿
17°30' M

Fig. 42

day. Sun and Venus t are aspected with Jupiter and Uranus. With Prince **Hendrik** (Fig.45) Sun and Uranus are close together (2/4 in the contact cosmogram), so that his Jupiter = Sun/Uranus, also indicates a happy change in life. In his case, Sun and Venus simultaneously transit the Sun, and Jupiter follows suit in the next few days. The trip through Danemark which the couple undertook after the wedding is reported to have gone smoothly.

Fig. 43

With persons who feel themselves united in love, there should be evidence of coincident configurations in the contact cosmogram which indicate common experiences or turns of fate. The prime object is to find such configurations and then to accommodate any joint efforts to the times when these points of contact are activated by favorable constellations.

Hence traditional astrology's practice of allowing an orb of $10°$ in comparing the horoscopes of couples is not correct, since the simultaneous resolution of certain configurations takes place in that case not only days but weeks and months apart. Responsible advice must be founded on correspondences as exact to the degree as possible.

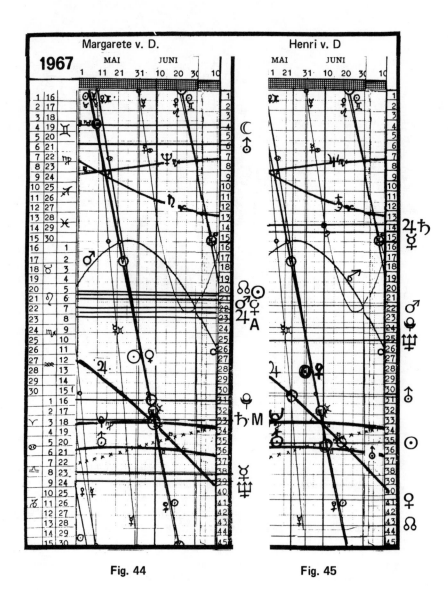

Fig. 44   Fig. 45

MARRIAGE CRISIS AND ATTEMPTED SUICIDE

We can outline the 1967 annual diagram of **Sigrid Bauer,** born on March 31, 1944, at 2 p.m. at 13° 30E and 49° N, as follows:

Saturn and Uranus transit the MC in January of 1967 and thus indicate unrest and trouble. The person in question would like to go her own way, but only encounters difficulties which cannot be properly coped with. In order to eliminate the necessity here of going through all the correspondences of the configurations at hand, I would like to draw your attention to the transit combinations in the appendix, which have been numbered for this purpose, Cf. TC 39 and 52.

In March, Saturn transits Mars (TC 31), Jupiter (TC 32) and Neptune (TC 35). All efforts are met with resistance, there are difficulties in achieving her own aims, and emotional depression and unbalance are the result.

Jupiter, apparently stationary, on the position line of Mercury at the same time allows for the development of new plans. But there is no release in tension under Uranus over Saturn (TC 46) and Piuto (TC 49). Concurrently, Pluto is involved in an aspect of several months' duration with Moon's Node (TC 76). For the time to come, associations with others can be of the greatest significance.

Very favorable Jupiter transits over Venus (TC 17) and Node (TC 24) develop in June, which can mean happiness in the relationship with the partner. However, Saturn over Sun (TC 27) and Moon (TC 28) is in direct contradiction, and from which we may conclude the possibility of estrangement.

Now the transits of Uranus over Saturn and Uranus repeat themselves, and Neptune maintains its aspect with the Ascendant for quite a while (TC 64). In September, a new clustering of critical aspects of Saturn over Sun and Moon and Uranus over MC (TC 52) results. Stress can increase. Jupiter over Sun (TC 14) and Moon (TC 15) can hardly provide an adequate compensation for Pluto over Saturn and Uranus at the end of September and the beginning of October. At this point, Mars over Saturn and Pluto also becomes involved (TC 7 and 8) and provides the native with a test of nerves.

These considerations coincide fairly precisely with the actual development of the case history. **Fritz Brandau** described this case in detail in the February issue of "Kosmobiologie", 2/1968, and presented his analysis. The facts are as follows:

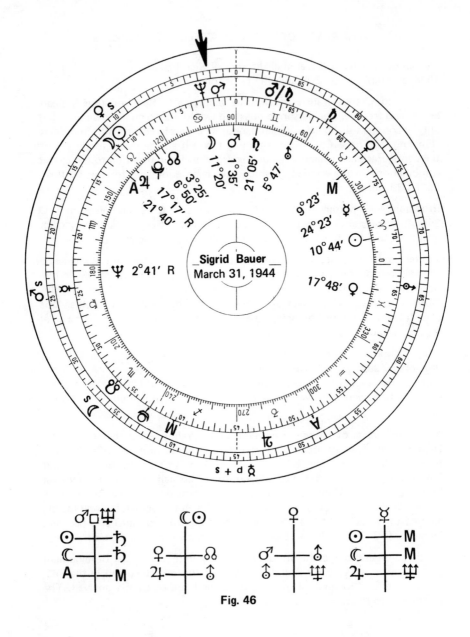

Fig. 46

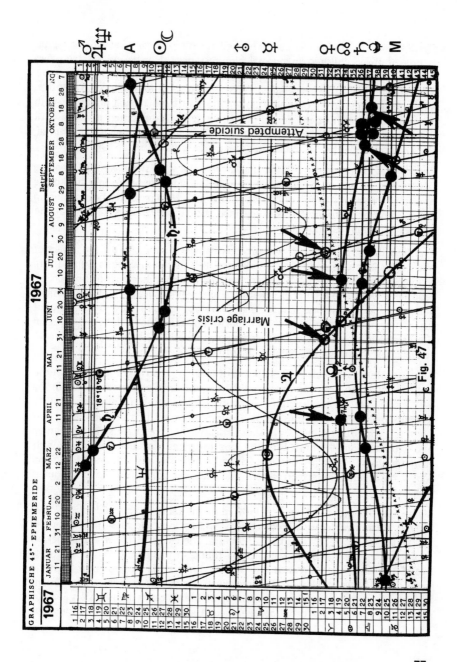

Fig. 47

Sigrid Bauer (the name has been changed for discretionary reasons) grew up as one of three children in normal circumstances. Her period started when she was 14 years of age and was always irregular. She married because she was expecting. For two years (since 1965) she regularly took the contraceptive. Since about July (but probably June) she had been having an affair with another man. Her husband found out about it and confronted his wife with the fact, and who then admitted to the affair. Her husband wanted a divorce, and an appointment with the lawyer was made for October 2, 1967.

Before they were to set off for the lawyer, the wife swallowed 30 sleeping tablets and fell asleep in the car. Her husband immediately brought her to the hospital. Treatment began on October 2nd at 3.15 p.m. Sixty hours later, in the evening of October 4th, she regained consciousness. She stated that she had acted completely on impulse.

The first thing to strike our eye on looking at the natal chart is the aspect of Mars with Neptune in the 90° circle, and this at the midpoints Sun/Saturn, Moon/Saturn, Ascendant/MC. Even these suffice to indicate emotional crises, especially when the feeling of isolation and loneliness are present; depressions and psychic unbalance could also develop, possibly as the result of disappointment. IMercury p: and Mercury s both turn up in this configuration simultaneously in 1967, indicating absent-mindedness, weak nerves (as a consequence of medicaments, alcohol, nicotine, caffeine, etc.).

Sun and Moon are decisive for matters of love and marriage and the relationship between man and woman; here they are square to one another and, in the 90° circle, are in conjunction. A happy love relationship should actually develop from Venus/Moon's Node = Jupiter/Uranus. In the year 1967, this planetary picture is joined by Venus. This means love (Venus) between man and woman (Sun/Moon). But the cosmos does not concern itself with marriage vows. Peculiarly enough, Saturn transits the position line of Sun and Moon twice and, in effect, severs the marriage bonds, and love is sought elsewhere.

Venus, as the planet of love, is located in the radix at the midpoints Mars/Uranus = Uranus/Neptune. From this results a strong and passionate excitability which is in great need of fulfillment. The cause of the irregular period beginning at the age of 14 can also be found in this configuration. In these years, Uranus s square Venus and Venus s square Mars opposition Neptune were due. Venus at Uranus/Neptune gives rise to the inclination to dream and idolize, totally ignoring the realities of life. Moon s conjunction Moon's Node = Venus/Saturn produce the inclination to adulterous relationships.

Mars s square Mercury leads to involvement in conflicts, and irresponsibility is intrinsic in Jupiter/Neptune.

We see from these observations that the directions together with the radix already gave an indication of what was subsequently triggered by the configurations in the annual diagram. Cosmobiological consultation would surely have helped the native to find the right path in the face of her troubles.

KING CONSTANTINE AND QUEEN ANNEMARIE

King **Constantine** and Queen **Annemarie** became engaged in February of 1963. In view of his father's death on March 6, 1964, the Crown Prince was unable to set an early date for the wedding. The marriage took place on September 18, 1964, in Athens. (Unfortunately, we only have the birth-dates of the partners and not their birth-hours as well.)

In the section from the annual diagram, the king's position lines have been heavily drawn, and those for the queen have been given as dotted lines. One point of contact is very obvious: the king's Venus and the queen's Mars coincide, in actual fact they form a square. Without considering the personal points, we only find a few transits for the day of the wedding. The wedding itself is, of course, only an external and formal affair, the actual union took place a few days later.

Very obvious, too, is that Sun, Mercury and Venus transit the mutual point of contact around the 8th of October (Fig.51). There were consequences of this love configuration, which can easily be checked on. October 8 is the 281st day of the year. (For this calculation we use the Tables of Events). Adding the usual 273 days of pregnancy to this, we get 55 days. Subtracting one year consisting of 365 days, we get a resulting 190 days. The 190th day of the year is July 9. Princess Alexia, the first child, was born on July 10, 1965.

The year 1967 was especially eventful for the royal couple (Fig.52). The coup d'état carried out by arch-conservative army officers occurred on April 21, on May 20 Crown Prince **Paul** was born, and on December 13, 1967, came the king's counter thrust, which failed, and he was forced to flee the country and was unable to return to his throne.

It is typical that at the birth of the Crown prince the Venus—Mars aspect (see (1) in Fig. 50) was triggered in the case of both partners by Sun and Mercury. Shortly after the birth, Jupiter transited one other mutual point, i.e. the king's Pluto and the queen's Node. Finally, Pluto approached for the last time the position line of Jupiter. The king was able to stay in power, and the officer's insurrection of April 21 was suppressed, to which end Jupiter over Sun also contributed. Pluto aspected with the queen's Saturn indicates her anxiety about the political situation. With the king, the persistent crisis is expressed in Neptune and Saturn twice transiting Uranus, Saturn over Mars twice becoming due, Uranus transiting Neptune and Saturn, and, finally, the approach of Neptune to Mars and Pluto to Neptune at the end of the year.

80

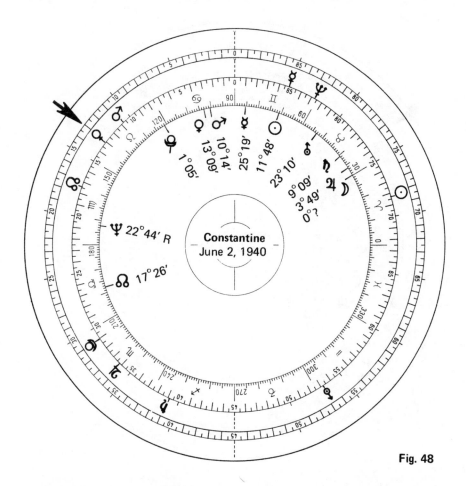

Constantine
June 2, 1940

Fig. 48

Neptune over Mars designates lack of willpower and ineffectiveness, especially since in the natal chart Mars is to be found at Sun/Saturn. Pluto over Neptune points to unusual problems and serious losses. Please note the many stellar bodies concentrated around Neptune and Saturn (and the queen's Uranus) around the 13th of December. Pluto, Mars, Sun are clustered here together, so that the king can be thankful that his escape was even successful. In the case of the queen, the apparently stationary Jupiter signals the success of the escape in face of general defeat and the loss of prestige and power.

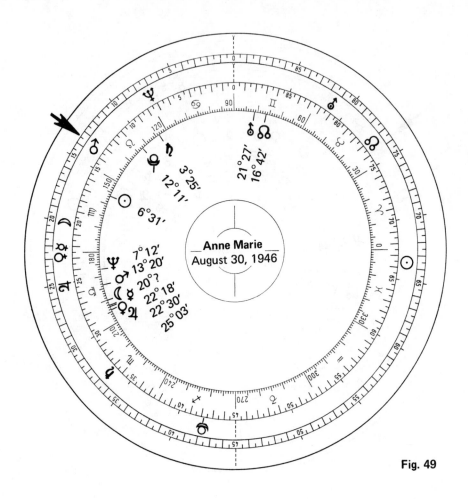

Anne Marie
August 30, 1946

Fig. 49

King Constantine and Queen Annemarie of Greece

Kontakt-Kosmogrammm für

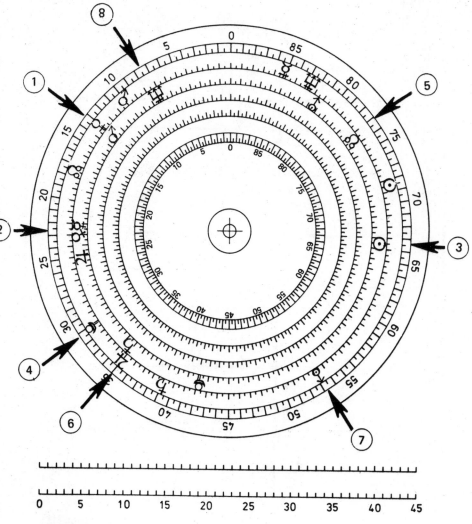

Formular KK
Entwurf : Reinhold Ebertin
© Copyright 1973 by   Ebertin Verlag Reinhold Ebertin D 7o8o Aalen/Württ.

Fig. 50

83

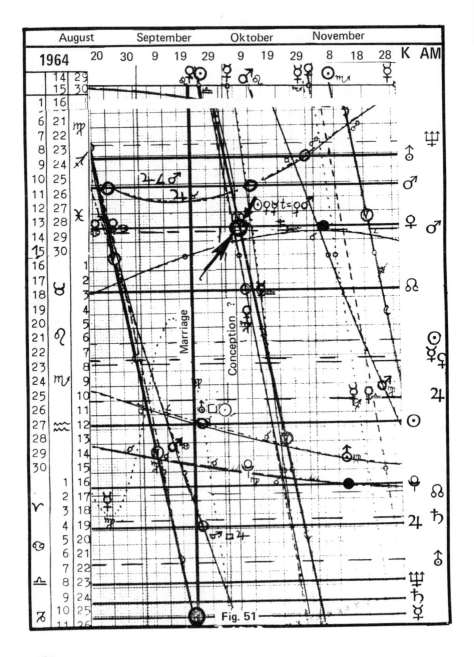

Fig. 51

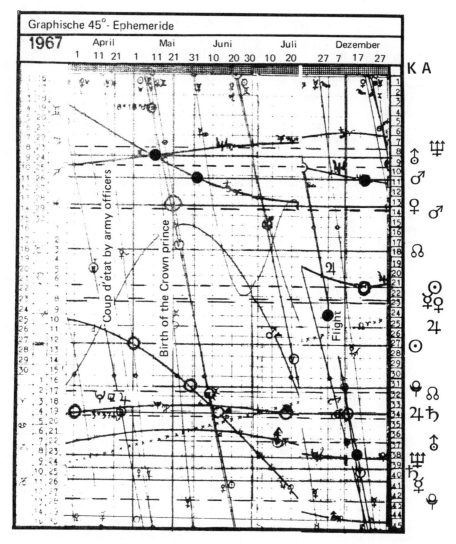

Fig. 52

WINNING IN THE LOTTERY

We present here an article by Mrs. **Gerta Laurent** from "Kosmobiologie", Vol. 35, No. 4, 1968, in which she writes as follows: "A woman, born on December 9, 1922, at 4.45 p.m. at 12° 29 E, and 50° 43 N, won the grand prize in the lottery on the weekend of April 2, 1960. It was only on the following Tuesday that she found out about it by reading the newspaper; her winnings amounted from 200,000 to 300,000 DM. This was the second week she had played this series of numbers. There was no big celebration with food and drink, but visits were made to relatives and large presents were bought for all. Also, a nice trip was made. As anyone will know, life on an engineer's pay is not filled with luxury. Now the couple had the possibility of buying their own home and new furnishings, as well as a larger car, and indulging in a trip to the Mediterranean every year, and of fulfilling other wishes. Seven years later, a new phase of "counting pennies" became necessary, in order to have something left for their old age."

I have pointed out repeatedly that the chances for winning in the lottery are not easy to calculate, and I would like to spare all those readers from disappointment who believe the cosmogram is a sure way of winning. It must be realized that there are a number of factors involved in such prizes:

1. First of all, the possibility of sudden monetary gains has to be present in the natal chart. One such configuration can be found in this case, Uranus = Jupiter/Pluto. This configuration can be interpreted as sudden (Uranus) gain (Jupiter/Pluto).

2. There have to be corresponding directions due for the year in question where gain is hoped for. This is also the case here, for in this year Sun s aspects with the Ascendant and Uranus. This indicates an unusual success or gain. In addition there is Mars p—135—Jupiter, Jupiter s = Sun (and Mercury) = Jupiter /Ascendant.

3. The potential and the directions should be triggered by transits in the annual diagram. This is also true here. Jupiter aspected with Neptune is implicative of success through speculation or gains without great effort (CSI 806). The Sun triggers not only Pluto but also Jupiter/Uranus, indicating a happy change in the financial circumstances (CSI 795 and 802). Saturn square Saturn has just been overcome.

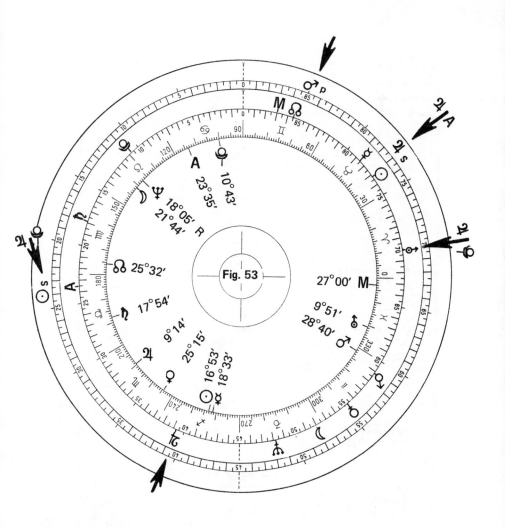

Fig. 53

By using the Graphic 45° Midpoint Ephemeris we can also ascertain the current midpoints. We find here Jupiter/Uranus—90—Uranus, which stimulates the configuration in the cosmogram and the solar directions. The axis of success, Mars/Jupiter transits the Sun, and Jupiter/Pluto crosses Mercury. Finally, Moon's Node also becomes part of a "good luck" aspect.

This should suffice to show how many factors are indeed at play in a case of some sudden gain.

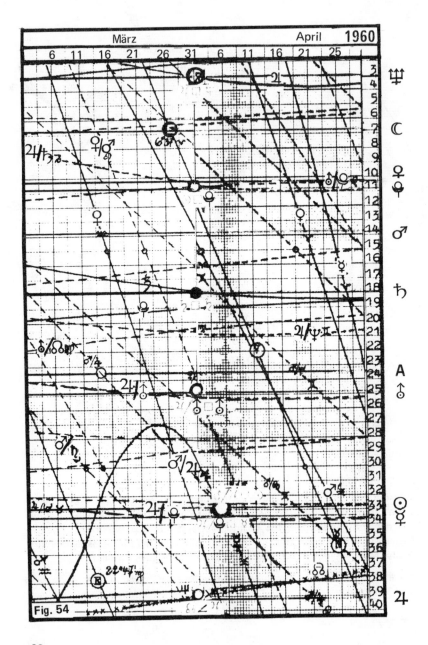

Fig. 54

TROUBLED YOUTH

Here in Aalen in February, 1971, three youths died within a few days of each other, deaths which might not have come about if the parents, with the aid of the Graphic Ephemerides, had been aware ahead of time of the danger threatening their children. Any large—scale investigation would show that there are many similar cases in other places as well.

I only had the birth—dates available, and yet, the impending crises are readily perceivable.

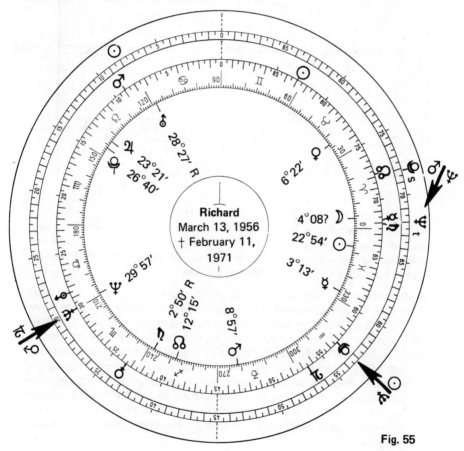

Fig. 55

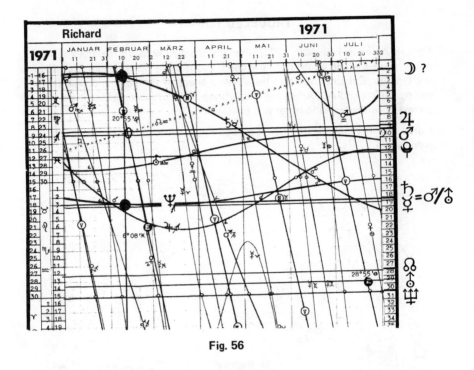

Fig. 56

Richard (all names have been changed), born on March 13, 1956, was a poor pupil and had had to repeat one year of school previously. At this time he was again fearful of getting bad grades, and on February 11th, tied a noose around his neck and hung himself from the door.

In the natal chart, Mercury and Saturn are quare. This would most likely mean that the boy is somewhat backward in his development and has a slow grasp of things. Mercury and Saturn are located at the midpoint Mars/Neptune, indicating not only nervous debility, but also the misuse of intoxicants, drugs, (hashish) etc., instability, feelings of inferiority, weakness. Due to Neptune at Mars/Jupiter, it must have been difficult for him to achieve his aims, and Pluto at Sun/Neptune points to strain due to emotional suffering, probably in connection with his failure at school. If these factors had been recognized in time, there would at least have been the possibility of removing him from the prepatory school and having him start on vocational studies more suited to his abilities.

90

The case is clearly mapped out in the Graphic Ephemeris. Transiting Neptune must already have aspected Saturn and Mercury the foregoing year. We see now Neptune's approach towards this configuration near the time of death. The boy must have at this time suffered under very deep depressions, to the extent that he no longer knew which way to turn. Since Mercury and Saturn in the natal chart are also located at Mars/Uranus, his act corresponds to the statements given in the CSI for these configurations (713, 761, 717): Placing great demands on one's nerves, premeditated test of strength, violence, energy directed towards separation, grave injury, absolute exhaustion from overtaxing one's energies.

Should the boy have been born during the morning hours, then Saturn would have aspected the Moon for the whole of January, which, as we know, can correspond to strong fits of depression.

Hubert, who was born on July 6, 1951, had already completely demolished three cars. On February 19, he crashed into a tree and died immediately.

The danger of mishap is already evident in the natal chart, where Mars is semisquare to Pluto = Saturn/Uranus. Applicable here are CSI 871 and 874: Occasional misuse of unusual energies, violence, demage due to force majeure.

Whereas in **Richard**'s case Mercury and Saturn were located at Mars/Neptune, Uranus is at this midpoint in this case, as a consequence of which sudden feebleness can be felt, especially when hashish is also indulged in.

Taking a look at the Graphic Ephemeris, we see the accident — if it was one — clearly before us. Transiting Saturn crossed Mars, which aspected Pluto and Saturn/Uranus, and therefore triggered the configuration mentioned. As is generally known, Saturn = Mars very frequently means death. Uranus is aspected with Jupiter and Sun, so that very likely a very good time was had during Carnival. The Sun transits Neptune, in which case we can presume that the youth was under the influence of drugs. Also, Mars was probably transiting the Moon, which corresponds to strong excitement as well as acts carried out unconsciously. The youth was no longer in control of the situation. It is also possible that he was in a depressed mood or was already ill, since the directed Saturn came to a halt at Neptune.

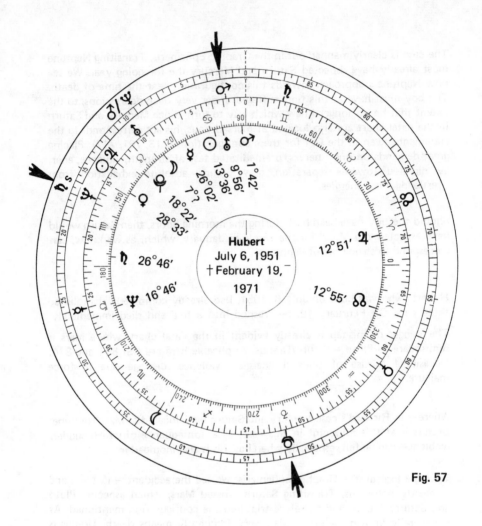

Hubert
July 6, 1951
† February 19, 1971

Fig. 57

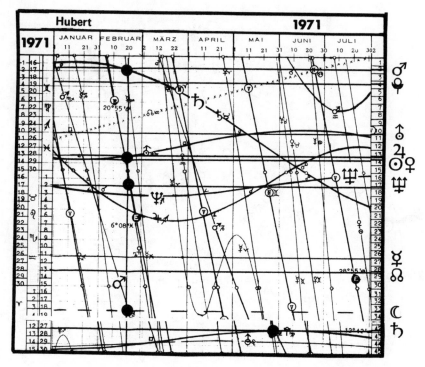

Fig. 58

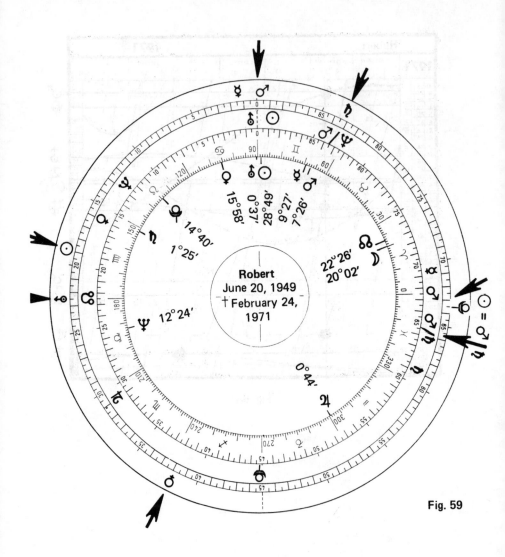

Fig. 59

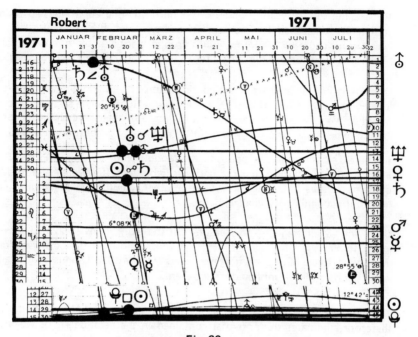

Fig. 60

Robert, the son of wealthy parents, was born on June 20, 1949, was found completely unclothed on February 24 and was probably murdered. He was heard in his room with another youth around three a.m. by his parents, who however did not detain him when he and the other boy left the house again.

Obvious in the natal chart is the configuration of Sun and Uranus, which is located opposite Pluto in the 90° circle. The latter is at the same time to be found at Mars/Moon's Node. These configurations themselves indicate some "tragic experience, severe physical suffering, violent dissolution of a group."

In the 90° circle, Mars is opposite the Moon's Node at Uranus/Pluto. This leads to the conclusion that the native is liable to suffer violence, a mishap or some serious injury at some time or other. Neptune at Mars/Pluto can lead to irreconciliability, malice, harm.

Using the calculating disc to measure out the elongations of 22° to correspond to the age of 22 years, we find that almost all the configurations mentioned above have been triggered. Mars s strikes Sun/Uranus = Pluto and hence signifies injury, mishap or tragic events.

The axis of Pluto-Uranus comes to a standstill at Mars and Moon's Node and therefore stimulates the potential contained in the natal chart for violence, mishap, injury. Sun s at Mars/Saturn indicates danger to life.

The potential and directions as mentioned are indeed triggered in the Graphic Ephemeris. Pluto t makes station over the complex of Sun, Pluto and Uranus, the square to the Sun is exact. Sun and Venus transit Saturn. Uranus approaches Neptune (=Mars/Pluto), signifying cruelty, violence, brutality. The native is also said to have taken hashish, so that he could quite easily become a victim of others.

Even if we do not calculate the directions, with the help of the Graphic Ephemerides we can still determine the fact of danger threatening all three youths.

Sole preoccupation with the Graphic Ephemerides is strictly out of the question, and with it, the dependence on the configurations alone. However, these examples should go to show the merits of occasionally orientating oneself by comparing the annual diagrams of the members of the family and making a note of the times when danger is possible. One could rightly say here that caution is the best cure.

THE TRANSIT COMBINATIONS (TC)

The evaluation of annual diagrams using the Graphic 45° Ephemerides as a basis requires a different technique. The object of these diagrams is not to grasp all the details, but rather to obtain a survey of an entire year and to combine the various indications given by the configurations.

I would like to avoid the word "interpretation" as far as possible, for we do not try making interpretations in the sense of traditional astrology, instead, we make use of the tendencies as substantiated repeatedly by similar configurations in numbers of cases.

As you will discover, the compilation of these TCs has been made in a different form from that used in my books, "Transits" and "The Combination of Stellar Influences." It has been found that the individual constellations can by no means be evaluated as purely positive or negative, or favorable or unfavourable. Rather, one should base one's considerations on a general classification and go on from there to determine in which direction a triggered configuration can have its effect. Let's take for instance the Uranus transits. These can, on occasion, cause a great deal of upset; they can, however, also bring a perfectly good turn in events or bring about a change in life. Or let's look at the configurations involving Moon's Node. These usually are applicable to relationships, but without any positive or negative nuance. An evaluation is only possible here when other configurations are also taken into account. Even if a stay in the hospital is under consideration, this does not necessarily have to be a bad thing, since it can contribute greatly to recovery.

The TCs of Sun, Moon, Mercury, and Venus have been omitted here, because these bodies generally are active in triggering other configurations. Of significance for an event are the slow—moving planets, although the directions, to which repeated reference has been made, should also not be overlooked.

My guidelines are intended only to serve as a kind of stimulation; everyone has to develop in experience on his own. Similarly, the native of the cosmogram in question is himself the best person to evaluate circumstances, once he has gained sufficient experience. After all, there always remains aspects which are part and parcel of the innermost person and which are not spoken out loud, but which can be essential to the evaluation. For this reason, no calculative analysis, comprehensive though it may be, can replace a face to face talk, at which opportunity the counsellor can ask about the resolution of particular configurations, in order to be better able to draw substantiated conclusions and give responsible advice.

The end—goal of our research is not only to study the correlations between cosmos and man, but also to make practical application of our knowledge in everday life.

Uppermost in importance is to redirect our aims from the mere prognostication of events, thus causing, under circumstances, suffering for the individual concerned; we should instead aim at drawing up guidelines as to behavior and attitudes appropriate to the eventual configurations, and teaching individuals how they, with the aid of the "cosmic information", can consciously guide their lives, master critical situations and make use of favorable opportunities.

Those who at the same time, work to improve themselves, smoothing out faults of character and developing themselves to worthy members of society, restraining negative urges and showing kindness to others, will perforce become harmonious individuals and successful persons. They will not easily be affected by adverse influences, but can experience true happiness under positive configurations.

The individual himself shapes his own destiny, the cosmic information only makes it easier for him to find the right path.

THE TRANSIT COMBINATIONS

have been numbered, so that in your analyses you need only refer to the corresponding number instead of having to give a complete description of the combination. Space has been purposely left between each TC to allow room for you to make your own notes.

TC 1   **MARS : SUN**

Intensified energy and enterprise promote the power of assertion, the ability to overcome difficulties, physical performance, and make it easier to attain one's goals. The unconscious or unthinking use of this energy can, because of precipitancy and impulsiveness, result in upset, conflict, incidents, error or mishap. The use of force, including injuries or surgical operations, is possible in the case of combinations with Uranus or Pluto. An increase in temperature can be expected with illnesses. Those with heart trouble should avoid all excitement.

TC 2   **MARS : MOON**

Energy and feeling are coupled in all activities. A lot can be attained when one does things with verve and interest. One should, however, not get upset and do anything without thinking it over beforehand, in order to preclude any disadvantages. Women may not feel well, especially at. New or Full Moon.

TC 3   **MARS : MERCURY**

Increased mental keenness is favorable for negotiations and discussions, leads to the realization of plans, and brings success due to eloquence. With some persons — depending on the cosmic state in the natal chart — upset and nervousness will manifest, and with others, this will mean aggressiveness and quarrelsomeness, criticism; and selfcontrol will be required.

TC 4   **MARS : VENUS**

A need for love, passionateness, impulsiveness may put in an appearance. This configuration is particularly involved in the act of conception, especially when the corresponding points of contact exist between the cosmograms of the two partners. A negative cosmic state can be conducive to extreme passionateness, tactlessness, impudence, lack of self—control. On occasion, menstruation can be of longer duration and the menstrual flow stronger.

TC 5   **MARS : MARS**

Increased energy leads to intensified activity and enterprise, and individual goals can be attained as a result of increased performance. One has to restrain oneself in order not to be ruthless or even violent. There is here a liability for mishap and injury, especially when other transits give indications of such.

TC 6   **MARS : JUPITER**

An optimistic attitude, a certain love of life, the spirit of enterprise, and creativity can lead to favorable decisions, good transactions and success. One can gain recognition or receive gifts. Many a problem can.be.solved more easily, and inhibitions and difficulties can be overcome. Only an arrogant and aggressive attitude can be of disadvantage in combination with corresponding configurations.

TC 7   **MARS : SATURN**

Intentions are met with resistance, and only through endurance and indefatigability can certain tasks be achieved. Arrogance, defiance, irreconcilability can only bring great disadvantages. This configuration may also be involved in bereavement or fateful events. Restraint and self—control · is required in all endeavors.

TC 8   **MARS : URANUS**

The desire for freedom and independence, obstinacy, and rebellion can lead to conflict. Sudden and, in the end effect, successful bursts of energy, are possible; however, there is the danger of overexertion, of injury and mishap. Mars and Uranus play a special role in cases of surgical operations. Special tests of nerves or strength may also be demanded. Great caution and reserve are especially required under this configuration. A surgical operation may prove to be necessary in the·case of illness.

TC 9   MARS : NEPTUNE

It is very likely that here the will to work and the spirit of enterprise are inhibited. This may be caused by emotional suffering, dissappointment, or even by some kind of poisoning, e.g. through mushrooms, spoiled food, or medicaments. One should by no means give free rein to discontent, moodiness, and feelings of inferiority. Intoxicants and stimulants should be avoided as much as possible. In some cases, this configuration can lead to criminal acts. An improper diet can bring about sickness and nausea.

TC 10   MARS : PLUTO

Very high performance is possible under this constellation, e.g. in sports; there is, however, also the danger of mishap and misfortune. Depending on individual disposition, this transit can evoke ruthlessness and violence, and also the suffering of brutality and violence. Caution and selfcontrol are imperative under this configuration.

This configuration relates to persons living and working together, in positive as well as negative terms, and hence its influence depends on the other configurations involved. This transit is also involved in matters of partnership, love, and marriage.

One attempts to assert oneself in the environment (family, place of work, etc.), to lead or compel others. Others will tend to react to an aggressive attitude with resistance, obstinacy, and general irritation. Conflicts should not end in physical violence. Self—restraint is better than provocation. (The question can always be put whether the Ascendant or the minute of birth are indeed precise.)

TC 13   **MARS : MIDHEAVEN**

The individual strives to realize his own thoughts and ideas, developing in the process a great deal of energy and goalconsciousness and evidencing the ability to make important decisions. Precipitant and impulsive action is to be avoided. Vocational problems can be solved.

TC 14   **JUPITER : SUN**

At this time, several possibilities for success exist : negotiations can run smoothly, contact with others made quickly, or one's emotional or physical state can improve. Arrogance and condescension towards others should be avoided, and restraint should be exercised in eating and drinking, especially of rich foods and alcoholic beverages, etc. Noticeable recovery from an illness may be the case. This and similar configurations can be conducive to a quick recovery after a surgical operation.

TC 15   **JUPITER : MOON**

Enthusiasm for another person or for some special plan is possible in an elated mood, one may also attract the benevolence of others, and with it may come the attainment of recognition or advantages. The contact with a loved one can be especially close and happy. The inclination to generosity and unnecessary expenditure should be kept within bounds. With men, this configuration frequently brings about the acquaintanceship with the future wife or the marriage itself.

TC 16   **JUPITER : MERCURY**

An especially keen mental and spiritual state should be taken advantage of for special plans, vocational goals, matters of organization, agreements or contracts. Trips can turn out well. This is a good configuration for exams or job applications.

TC 17 JUPITER : VENUS

At this time, one can appear to be an especially attractive and sincere person, thus gaining friends. This can also mean an especially good contact with the opposite sex, a contact which eventually could also lead to marriage. A propitious time for purchasing clothing, jewellery, objects d'art, or for the pursuit of any special hobby. Artists can gain much applause and recognition.

TC 18 JUPITER : MARS

With an energetic and positive attitude it is possible to conduct successful negotiations, to assert oneself in a community or group, to settle conflicts and differences, to bring about important decisions, to develop oneself more freely and thus perhaps to commence on a new phase of life. At times, vocational differences or legal conflicts can be the case.

On days when one can justifiably feel content and much good is coming one's way, it is advisable to give full rein to one s positive powers, to attain recognition and take advantage of opportunities, and by no means to indulge in pleasure for pleasure's sake, e.g. overly rich eating and drinking which can be harmful to health.

Perseverance and patience can aid in overcoming any difficulties; the consciousness of fulfilling one's duties towards oneself can add to self—confidence. Should things not be going according to desire or plan, it is better to take a wait—and—see stance rather than to force things. In order to keep in good health, it is important to pay close attention to diet and not to do anything wrong there. Under such configurations one is completely on one's own and cannot expect much help from elsewhere.

TC 21   **JUPITER : URANUS**

Inner tensions can be released suddenly, new perceptions and points of view are possible, one strives towards change or is subject to such, due to circumstances. A quick grasp of the situation can enable one to meet all demands and take quick advantage of opportunities. Inner unrest or perhaps some revolutionary attitudes should not result in tactlessness or exaggeration. One should try to settle and not intensify conflicts. This configuration can also mean "sudden good fortune or happiness" after times of duress.

TC 22   **JUPITER : NEPTUNE**

One indulges in making plans, giving way to all sorts of ideas and exploring one's imagination, but there is the danger here of getting involved in speculative affairs or of being disappointed. During this time, one should remain clearheaded and not let oneself be misled or tempted, and one should always be realistic in attitude. Those who do not remain steadfast can become involved in unpleasant conflicts. The statements "undeserved luck" or "money earned without effort" are just as rare as true coincidence.

TC 23   **JUPITER : PLUTO**

The strong urge to advance can lead to special recognition or success. One's own attitude, however, should be the main contributing factor to taking the proper advantage of the chances offered. One's behavior should be such as to preclude any kind of "backlash". Should other positive configurations be involved, unusual advancement may be possible.

TC 24   **JUPITER : MOON'S NODE**

Due to great adaptability, it is possible to come into contact with others more easily, to make acquaintances on a social or vocational basis, to work well with others and to develop good fellowship, or, also, to take on leadership in a group.

TC 25   **JUPITER : ASCENDANT**

A good relationship with the environment can develop; one is better able to maintain contacts in the environment as well as being interested in the beautification of the environment. Good relations with others often leads to recognition or success. During this time, existing conflicts or differences can be more easily settled. Success can ensue from some public activity.

TC 26   **JUPITER : MIDHEAVEN**

A harmonious emotional and spiritual attitude can make relations with others easier, one has new goals, or one is able to better one's position. One should be energetic in the proper exploitation of opportunities. Of great importance is whether Jupiter is moving slowly or quickly over Midheaven or its aspects.

TC 27   **SATURN : SUN**

It is possible for greater difficulties, family problems and worries, disturbances in health and development, and lack of initiative to arise. In this event, it is advisable first to concentrate on the most important matters, to step back and quietly analyse the present situation and how it can be handled. Contact or cooperation with others should not be the result of compulsion, so as to avoid further alienation or separation. In the case of digestive problems, a light and natural diet is preferable.

TC 28   **SATURN : MOON**

Outward events, inner tension and inhibition, feelings of interiority, can give rise to poor relations and tension. There is no point in indulging in one's moods of depression, but rather, one should try to find a way to achieve more self—confidence, to come to terms emotionally with the inevitable and unavoidable, and to release oneself from inner isolation. In a short time, the world can put on entirely different face and one will have more verve. There may be some disturbances involving the bodily fluids, and urination should be increased.

TC 29 SATURN : MERCURY

If there are any difficult problems to be solved, do not be precipitant, instead, approach all problems with greater patience and perseverance than usual. Errors are more easily made by those who during this time are unable to concentrate well and are not clear—headed and objective in their thinking. Difficulties with others, alienation or separation can result from the insistence on one's own standpoint or a biased attitude. A trip can often provide a good solution. The intellectually—minded person should indulge in philosophical considerations.

TC 30 SATURN : VENUS

Temporary sexual inhibition, lack of satisfaction, misunderstandings, jealousy can lead to disillusionment, to disappointment or alienation in regard to loved ones or to friends. Emotional conflict can also be linked to organic disturbances. Special attention should be paid to glandular and kidney activity. With women, abdominal disorders, and with men, trouble with the prostate gland are possible.

TC 31 SATURN : MARS

In the face of unusual difficulties, do not despair, but muster up all the energy possible to master the situation. Intentions will meet with resistance, but this serves as a test of one's own strength and potential. Events may occur which are beyond personal control, where one has no other choice but to adapt oneself to the conditions. There is the possibility of news of someone's death. All use of force should be avoided, and this includes operative intervention, setting of joints, intensive massage, etc.

TC 32 SATURN : JUPITER

When things are not going according to plan, it is necessary to apply a great deal of energy, effort, and patience to achieve one's goals despite the difficulties. One should never lose faith in one's own abilities. In a short time, the obstacles will be overcome, and life will be easier to master. In the case of illness, severe physical exertion and the overtaxing of one's energies are to be avoided; proper care should be taken of one's health to promote recovery. A change in residence or locality or in relations with others can occur. Digestive trouble can be prevented by eating light foods.

There may be signs of one phase of life ending and another beginning. Certain difficulties can arise as a result, but once these have been overcome, life will have become easier again. In such times, it is wise to pause awhile, just as the wanderer stops to take a "breather" after climbing to the hilltop and then steps on at a lighter pace. Turning points are most likely to occur in the seven years' rhythm with conjunction, square, opposition.

One is impatient, on the one hand, to achieve a particular goal, and on the other, one comes face to face with difficulties in this connection. In a state of inner tension, one has to exert all one's energy to overcome the obstacles without upsetting the environment or without getting involved in personal conflicts or disputes. One must, however, resist all uses of force and restrictions in individual development and activity.

TC 35   **SATURN : NEPTUNE**

In the case of emotional suffering, one should take care of one's physical condition and health; when in poor health, one should avoid all emotional stress in order to recover. One will be compelled to concentrate on one's own self, and the effort will have to be made to overcome a particular crisis. Courage and confidence will aid in mastering every situation. A natural diet can alleviate illness.

TC 36   **SATURN : PLUTO**

Great effort may have to be expended in order to achieve a certain goal, and one may often find oneself dependent on external difficulties or events which are no fault of one's own. Self—discipline must be exercised and some sacrifices made. All thoughts of being a martyr should be put aside and new problems faced with confidence. Relaxing exercises and a lot of sleep can add to one's feeling of well—being.

SATURN : MOON'S NODE

It is not always easy living together with others and adapting oneself. It is, however, at times better to show goodwill and not let alienation or a rupture come about. It is also possible that one's ties with others are based on suffering or difficulties. If one can, no meetings should be held in such periods and special arrangements should be made. It may also turn out that a stay in some institution will prove to be necessary, where one will be in close contact with the ill or emotionally upset.

SATURN : ASCENDANT

When feeling restraint with regard to the environment or when suffering with others, the energy must be found to master the situation and to instill courage in oneself. At times, voluntary self—restraint is better than the possible development of an alienation or rupture.

TC 39   **SATURN : MIDHEAVEN**

There are times at which one feels restraint in all regards, when difficulties can only be overcome with great effort, and when one sees no possibilty of advance or progress. The only thing to do at such times is to gain experience, exercise self—restraint, do one's duty and wait for brighter prospects. The day bringing great relief will come, and rapid progress will again be possible. One should not forget the fact that the body, too, needs a respite in order to revitalize.

TC 40   **URANUS : SUN**

Inner unrest feeds the urge for changes in vocational life or alterations in the conditions of life. Upsets involving others are likely. It is also possible for external events or causes to enforce some change. Depending on disposition, an inclination for nervous disorders, heart trouble or danger through accidents may be at hand. Diversions and recreation should be sought or changes made in one's abode, if these are likely to be conducive to relaxation and a soothing atmosphere.

TC 41   URANUS : MOON

Intense, emotional excitablility urges one to release oneself from tension and to realize ideas and plans. One has the strong will to get one's own way and to fulfill certain ambitions. It will prove necessary to have to keep one's emotions under continuous control. Differences could easily arise in living and working together with others. Ambition can be the wrong trigger for action. Women should watch out for menstrual disorders.

TC 42   URANUS : MERCURY

A person of ingenuity, having new ideas and measuring up to any situation. One would prefer to do many things at once and has to control oneself in order not to become nervous or be rash. A great liking for diversity and stimulation and many—sided activity. This inner unrest can best be overcome by pursuing one's many interests.

TC 43

URANUS : VENUS

In connection with relationships with the opposite sex there is a potential intensification — at times impulsive in character — of emotion and feeling. One is more readily able to make contacts, is well—liked and loves strongly and deeply. Thoughts of progenity. For creative persons (artists) exceptional creativity and productivity are possible. Extravagant inclinations should be controlled.

TC 44

URANUS : MARS

An unusual intensification of energy leads to increased performance; if this energy is misused, there is imminent danger of precipitancy, injury and mishap. An operation can in the case of illness prove to be necessary.Obstinacy, urge for independence and freedom of movement will frequently make their appearance, depending on existing circumstances and conditions. It is better to not always want one's own way.

TC 45   **URANUS : JUPITER**

At this time, there could be a sudden release of inner tensions, and one can attain new perceptions and achieve unexpected recognition, success, or there could be changes in one's circumstances. Good opportunities should not be missed; however, one should not have only material advantages in mind.

TC 46   **URANUS : SATURN**

On the one hand there is the urge to do something special and different, and on the other there are great inhibitions to be overcome. This results in a state of tension which has to be resolved in some way. One should beware of exciting undue controversy or of rebelling against others or behaving tactlessly. One will be better able to handle a situation through exercising self-control and through consideration rather than through the use of force.

TC 47   **URANUS : URANUS**

One is in all probability at the end of one phase of life and at the beginning
of a new period. This transition will take a long time to complete itself, and
one will only become gradually aware of the inner change; there will be
unrest and conflict to struggle against until one is again secure in the new
circumstances. This is especially true for the time around the 21st, 42nd,
63rd, and 84th year of life.

TC 48   **URANUS : NEPTUNE**

One often suffers because of one's emotional balance and is sensitive,
unclear in one's thoughts and is unable to make decisions, and experiences
disappointment — at times detrimental gossip — and one's relations with
others can easily be disturbed if one does not have oneself under continuous
control. At times, one can also experience an intensification of the unconscious forces, often expressing itself in dreams. However, one should
always try to remain objective and realistic in one's thinking in order not to
be misled. Disturbances in the organic rhythms should be quickly attended
to.

TC 49   **URANUS : PLUTO**

Making exceptional efforts, one would like to achieve great aims, carry out innovations, create new conditions of life, whereby one may often be confronted with crucial situations where one is forced to make decisions. External circumstances and force majeure may also at times play an important part, bringing about new conditions. Reformers and revolutionaries find their way when other positive aspects are involved.

TC 50   **URANUS : MOON's NODE**

There could be unrest or incidents in communal life or in work with others which could lead to upset or changes. One should do everything to avoid differences and conflicts. In most cases, it is advisable to adjust.

TC 51   **URANUS : ASCENDANT**

One tries to gain more influence over the environment and would like to make certain changes, to make contact with others, but one should also be aware of the possibility of incidents occurring suddenly. One should be in good control of oneself and be able to quieten down, in order to avoid disputes with others. One should always keep in mind the possibility of changes or incidents in the environment.

TC 52   **URANUS : MIDHEAVEN**

One would like to go one's own independent way, pursue new aims in life, achieve success and advancement, do new things. Frequently, a change in one's vocation or in one's conditions of life is brought about at this time. However, every venture should be carefully considered beforehand to avoid making any mistake. Vocational changes should only be planned when this configuration is followed up by very positive aspects.

TC 53   **NEPTUNE : SUN**

Being subject to moods, impressionability, susceptibility can easily lead to disharmony through or in relation with others, also to great disappointments, health disorders or disinclination to work. In this state, one would like to let oneself go, indulge in plans and dreams, and one can easily lose contact·with reality. Therefore, one should endeavor to free oneself from this negative phase and above all to fulfill one's obligations. Great disadvantages can result from personal indulgence.

TC 54   **NEPTUNE : MOON**

At this time, one is full of inspiration and premonition, one's imagination is especially active, but at the same time one is in danger of being deceived, of being unable to differentiate between appearances and reality, and even of being overly influenced by others. One tries to empathize with others, but feels oneself to be misunderstood and dissatisfied. One has to struggle against instability and weakness, health disorders may also be involved; the circulation should be stimulated, not through pills, which can be harmful at this time, but through exercise, massage etc.

NEPTUNE : MERCURY

With great imagination and many ideas one makes a lot of plans and is very perceptive, however, one has at this time little real energy to realize one's aims right away. One must beware of deceiving oneself and of making wrong judgements and acting prematurely. Experiences with others are not always the best and one should not wholly trust anyone. One should fight against nervous sensitivity. The actor is well able to do his mask, the writer is inspired, and the criminally inclined able to deceive and cheat.

TC 56 **NEPTUNE : VENUS**

Ideals and desires are difficult to realize and fulfill, one longs for love and also tends to idolize, demanding more of the partner than he can fulfill. There is danger of disappointment and disillusionment. There may also be the inclination for perversity. Beware of intoxicants, nicotine, drugs, etc.

TC 57 NEPTUNE : MARS

Despite irritability, moodiness, discontent, feelings of inferiority, and poor health, one should try to maintain one's usual level of performance and to avoid any conscious disruption in one's contact with others. Errors can easily result from the lack of energy and definite plans. The misuse of intoxicants and pills, etc., in the effort to "pep up" can be hazardous. Take special care against infections, since the body is at this time especially susceptible to poisons of all kinds.

TC 58 NEPTUNE : JUPITER

In every endeavor one should try to seek clarity and not let oneself be dissuaded from objectivity by others or by some enthusiastic outpourings. Loose and unstable behavior can give rise to gossip and scandal; there can be losses due to false speculation; the wrong diagnosis can result in improper treatment. Only be convinced by actual facts. At times, this configuration is also indicative of good fortune, such as winning the lottery, when the corresponding tendency is contained in the natal chart.

TC 59   **NEPTUNE : SATURN**

One gains experience and perception even from unpleasant situations and emotional suffering. In examining one's own self, one should by no means indulge in discontent and depression, but rather, be keenly aware of the reality of things and try to master things through a positive attitude. There is the possibility of illness, and one should therefore take precautionary measures or at the first signs, call a doctor. Those who are always annoyed at something are a source of satisfaction for others, and those who do not let themselves get annoyed will annoy those who begrudge them.

TC 60   **NEPTUNE : URANUS**

One should try, through broadening one's scope and looking at problems from many sides, to avoid onesidedness and bias. Also, to withdraw oneself from the influence of others, to overcome one's feelings of insecurity and lack of clarity, and to put on a clear and consistent attitude in one's relations with others, in order not be unduly subject to their influence. One can easily become the object of gossip and rumors. Special caution is to be taken in the case of parapsychological experiments and in associating with mediums, members of a sect, and "miracle people".

NEPTUNE : NEPTUNE

One is broadminded, receptive to new impressions, one tends to contemplate, one indulges in one's imagination. If in all of this one does not maintain the perception for what is real and actual, there is danger of misguidance. Pay attention to Neptune's cosmic condition in the natal chart.

NEPTUNE : PLUTO

One is burdened with unusual problems and endeavors, one can become subject to peculiar emotional states, but one can also attain special spiritual perceptions. Unconscious forces or even supernatural phenomena can become manifest. However, one must try always to remain clear—headed. Those who use intoxicants and the like to "keep themselves going" can easily become addicted. Health disorders with causes difficult to ascertain, can occur.

TC 63

One has difficulty in adjusting oneself to communal life. One tends to distrust others and is easily disappointed by others. Frequently, one forms wrong ideas about others or associations. Relationships can be undermined.

TC 64

One can become unclear about one's relations with others and with one's environment, and can experience breach of faith or disappointment. One has to draw upon all of one's energy to assert oneself and maintain one's position, and should not let oneself be misled. One can disappoint or be disappointed.

TC 65   **NEPTUNE : MIDHEAVEN**

When feeling insecure and unsure about things, one should limit one's endeavors and bide one's time until certainty is again present and one can make
decisions with assurance. One should check oneself for wrong ideals and
should not let faith in oneself or abilities be undermined by others. One
should be able to overcome disappointment and loss.

TC 66   **PLUTO : SUN**

Depending on the general circumstances it is possible to assert oneself, to
achieve a better position or realize one's aims. The possible effects extend
over a period of up to two years. One should guard oneself against fanaticism and overestimating oneself. If the natal sun is poorly positioned, one
should not let oneself be the martyr.

PLUTO : MOON

One is rich, and at times extreme, in feeling, is energetic and enthusiastic, and has very definite aims to be realized. However, those who exceed the bounds of their capabilities or self—imposed limits, or who act impulsively, or give too little consideration to others, will have to deal with strong opposition and emotional suffering. One should always try to maintain emotional equilibrium and not go from one extreme to the other.

PLUTO : MERCURY

It is possible to influence others through speech or writing, to turn every situation to good use, to proceed diplomatically and with cleverness, to attain recognition, and in certain vocations to start an advertising campaign. Over-estimation of one's powers can lead to nervous disorders.

TC 69   PLUTO : VENUS

An unusually strong power of attraction and strong feelings of love can result in intense experiences with the partner which occasionally exceed the normal, and at the same involve great emotional tension. Lovers should therefore carefully consider whether or not they could remain together a whole lifetime, and be objective despite the strong physical attraction. Namely, when this configuration has passed, the relationship of the partners can take on an entirely different face. The sexual tie should not be the sole deciding factor.

TC 70   PLUTO : MARS

There is the possibility of developing unusual power and energy and therefore of increasing one's performance and efficiency, and of achieving success on the incentive of one's ambitions. But the misuse of energy can make one brutal and cruel or one must suffer some interventions in one's life, such as is possible in the case of an accident or surgical operation. With politicians there is the danger of assassination.

An exceptional striving for power over others, or for wealth, can to a certain degree, depending on circumstances, be fulfilled. Some considerable vocational successes are in the offing if natal Jupiter is favorably positioned and good directions are due simultaneously.

Only with great tenacity and perseverance will it be possible to meet all demands. If one is not careful, one could be cheated of success in one's work, but here, the conditions of the times also have to be taken into consideration. This may come into effect, if one is in danger of being involved in some natural catastrophe, mass catastrophe, or war. One should oneself avoid the use of force. This configuration can be recognized a long time ahead, so that the necessary precautions can be taken. One should take special care of one's health.

TC 73   PLUTO : URANUS

With great effort and with the expenditure of much energy, one can achieve great aims, carry out innovations, create new conditions of life, and also be compelled to make decisions. One should avoid excitement, upset, and potential mishaps. With a positive cosmic condition of Uranus, changes, innovations, reforms can be carried out successfully.

TC 74   PLUTO : NEPTUNE

One is concerned with unusual problems or fantastic ideas, but one achieves clarity only with difficulty; it is better to wait before doing something until one is completely sure about things. One will on occasion have painful remembrances of earlier actions or experiences and will have to steel oneself to overcome the past. Emotional confusion should not be dampened by intoxicants, etc., which could only lead to addiction. One should be cautious in one's association with cranks and members of a sect.

PLUTO : PLUTO

One is at the end of one life phase and at the beginning of a new one. The transition takes altogether two years, and at first it means special problems or difficulties until one has come to terms with the new conditions. Generally, only a semisquare is possible, rarely a square. The decisive factor is the cosmic condition in the radix.

TC 76   **PLUTO : MOON'S NODE**

Associations or cooperation with others can become of great significance for future life. If, however, other critical configurations are involved at this time, one can share with others a strange fate or be forced to some mutual destiny (karmic link).

TC 77   PLUTO : ASCENDANT

One has the great desire to assert oneself in one's environment, to have an important role in one's vocation or to make special acquaintances and associations. However, one should act in such a way as not to unnecessarily provoke controversy or opposition, if one does not feel adequate the situation.

TC 78   PLUTO : MIDHEAVEN

Unusual aims also demand unusual energy and effort. At this time it is possible to take a great step forward, to attain the corresponding position, and parallel to inward changes, to undertake changes in the external circumstances. It is also possible for outward events to signify as a turn of fate. Those who have climbed to the peak should take care that they do not tumble. Close attention should be paid to the cosmic condition of the natal Midheaven.

One can enter into spiritual or physical (love) associations, or relations are with the public (newspaper articles, political party, the authorities).

One feels oneself spiritually allied with others. For a man this can mean the association with a woman, for a woman, the association with other women (women's club).

TC 81   **MOON'S NODE : MERCURY**

One exercises the exchange of thoughts with others or feels oneself spiritually allied, or participates in, common interest groups.

TC 82   **MOON'S NODE : VENUS**

This configuration is significant of a friendship or a love relationship. One cares about other people.

TC 83   **MOON'S NODE : MARS**

One allies oneself with others through the bonds of fellowship, collaboration or partnership.

TC 84   **MOON'S NODE : JUPITER**

One has good relations with others, one is promoted and supported by others, and one experiences joint successes.

TC 85   **MOON'S NODE : SATURN**

One feels ill at ease in close contact with others, one is disinclined to adjust, isolates oneself. One can also feel inhibited because of others or one is linked with others through emotional suffering (grief). Estrangements should be avoided.

TC 86   **MOON'S NODE : URANUS**

There will be frequent experiences with others, one becomes nervous, disquieted, upset because of others, there is disharmony in communal life, and one should compel oneself to selfcontrol.

One expects too much of others, is accordingly disappointed, personal dislike develops, and relationships are undermined. Alertness and intellectual and spiritual superiority help in avoiding disappointments.

TC 88   MOON'S NODE : PLUTO

One can feel oneself somehow bound to the masses, one shares in some mass fate, experiences some mass event. For a big industrialist this can mean the association with large concerns. Karmic — predestined — links also result.

TC 89   **MOON'S NODE : MOON'S NODE**

This configuration can be indicative of associations with others, of large meetings, of relatives.

TC 90   **MOON'S NODE : ASCENDANT**

Relations with others, acquaintanceships, cooperation with others can be involved here.

Relationships with others are individual in character due to common attitudes, ideals or aims.

Heavenly Bodies is the collective description of the Sun, Moon and the Planets. When in astrology, Sun and Moon are referred to as planets, this is obviously incorrect. The Sun is not a planet but a fixed star, neither is the Moon a planet but a satellite of the earth.

K 1 and **K 2** are abbreviations used for the two charts combining the 360°-circle with the 90°-circle. K 1 may be used as pocket size edition for charts with the size of the illustrations in this book. K 2 is a larger work chart intended for use with the dial.

m = abbreviation for male, w = abbreviation for female or woman (the translator has adhered to the German abbreviation for "männlich" = m, and "weiblich" = w in order to comply with the symbols used in the illustrations).

Malefics: this is a term that was used to describe planets whose action was said to be detrimental (Mars, Saturn) to differentiate them from the **Benefics** that — according to "the old belief in the stars" — were favourably disposed towards humanity. For us these fatalistic conceptions are now defunct. However, it is difficult to find an appropriate substitute. It would be better to speak of negative and positive, although we have to realize that every "nature" contains positive and negative elements in varying proportions.

MC = M = Medium Coeli refers to the point of culmination or meridian, which at the moment of birth, or of an event, is at a vertical angle to the (birth) place. Within the cosmogram, the letter M is to be preferred, but in the text we have used MC (similar as with A = AS) in order to avoid mix-ups.

Midpoints are angular relationships, in which one factor forming an axis is equidistant to two other factors, one on each side, — measured on the degree-circle. Mathematically, the middle factor is in the halfsum of the positions of the other two factors calculated from 0° Aries.

Naibod Arc is the mean daily movement of the Sun, which is about 57° to $1^\circ01'$.

Nature of the Heavenly Bodies: without reference to the various deities whose names they bear, experience has shown that each planet has different qualities or that they "reveal" themselves in different ways. Even popular language for instance denotes Mars as fiery, Saturn as cold, Venus as lovely. Under the "nature of the heavenly bodies" we understand their qualities as these have been determined by experience.

Orb: the angular relationships of the planets are not only valid when exact to the minute, a certain deviation or "orb" on either side is allowed. With the aspects 3°, 4° and 5°, with midpoints 1 1/2° are allowed. In traditional astrology orbs of up to 15° are acceptable but this is untenable.

p = progressive: the progression of the heavenly bodies (as directions) is calculated according to the measure of 1 day after birth corresponding to one year of actual life. Therefore, these types of directions are called progressive and the abbreviation used is p. (The author differentiates between progressed aspects p and solar-arc directions s. The abbreviation for the solar-arc directions is s for "solar arc".)

r = Radix = Root: this refers to the birth cosmogram, to distinguish it from other planetary configurations (p, s, t).

Release: once certain configurations, structures, etc. have been found in the cosmogram, one will wish to know the time when the tendencies shown in the birth configuration are likely to mature, that is when they will be released (or manifested or resolved).

s instead of the abbreviation "v" used hitherto, standing for "vorgeschoben" (= advanced), it is preferable to use "s" to indicate advanced factors based on "solar-arc".

Solar Arc is that arc of the zodiac which the Sun traverses in a given time. The daily advance of the Sun corresponds to one year of life. The other factors of the birth-chart are advanced by this same arc.

Structure Picture: this could be called composite picture, containing of the various structural elements emerging from the "cosmic condition" of the individual factors.

Symbols are the emblems denoting the heavenly bodies; for instance a circle with a dot in the centre represents the Sun, the crescent represents the Moon etc. Today these symbols are no longer to be considered as having symbolic meaning, because the planetary signs have been derived from Greek letters.

t = transiting: this is the abbreviation for a moving planet (according to the movement in the daily ephemeris) contrary to the fixed positions of the heavenly bodies at the moment of birth. The term "transits" is also used for the passage of the t-planets over the birth positions and their angular points.

v = "vorgeschoben" (see "s").

RECOMMENDED LITERATURE:

Reinhold Ebertin, **Transits**. What Day is Favorable for Me?, Aalen, 1971. This is recommended as a supplement to the book at hand.

Dr. **Fidelsberger,** Die Kosmobiologie ist bewiesen!, **Kosmobiologie,** August 1969.

The journal "**Kosmobiologie**" and its supplement, "**Kosmischer Beobachter**" offer current and practical examples using the Graphic 45° Ephemeris.

Reinhold Ebertin, **The Combination of Stellar Influences,** published since 1940 in many editions and revisions, is a must for the evaluation of the structural pictures as well as the transits and directions.

Reinhold Ebertin, **Direktionen,** Mitgestalter des Schicksals, introduction to the computation and evaluation of the annual directions.

Reinhold Ebertin, **Lebensdiagramme**, the method outlined here makes it possible to survey a life—span of 60 years using the solar arc directions and progressions.

Reinhold Ebertin, **Die kosmische Ehe**, a practical text—book on partner relationships.

Reinhold Ebertin, **The Contact Cosmogram.**

A comprehensive leaflet describing our publishing program is available on request.

Ebertin — Verlag, D—7080 Aalen/Württ., Postfach 1223

AIDS TO SETTING UP THE ANNUAL DIAGRAM

The transcription of the positions to the graphic 45° ephemeris is made easier when the cosmogram has been cast on Form C 2 (in pads of 10 and 50 sheets.) This chart form is also necessary for the determination of midpoints. Supplementary to this one also needs the **workboard**, available in various models.

The large workboard is made of cardboard and includes calculating disc and bolt for holding the chart form in place for the exact determination of the midpoints.

The universal magnetic workboard has many and various applications. On removal of the bolt and the calculating disc the graphic ephemerides can be inserted in the clamp and with the aid of the ruler included in the package exactly aligned. The ruler can be moved from the top to the bottom, it will always remain exactly horizontal. There is a special leaflet giving exact instructions on how to use the workboard.

The Graphic 45—Degree Ephemerides, format approx. 8 1/2 x 10'', available in pads of 10 sheets. Single sheets cannot be supplied. There is always need for several, since one also has to set up annual diagrams for the members of the family or for friends, in order to make comparisons and relevant observations.

The Graphic 45—Degree Midpoint Ephemerides are larger in size, are more precise and also indicate the current midpoints, which are often of decisive importance. Up to now, the midpoint ephemerides were issued in quarterly sheets. At present, the attempt is being made to comprise one half year on one 8 1/2 x 10'' page. Two sheets comprise one year. One pad contains 5 ephemerides = 10 sheets.

Transcriptions of your own natal charts to the chart form and a graphic ephemeris will be undertaken by the **Ebertin Verlag** for a certain fee. Please request brochures from the **Ebertin Verlag.**

Section from the graphic 45—degree midpoint ephemeris. At the end of July we see, for instance, that Mars is located at the midpoint Jupiter/Moon's Node. Accordingly, Mars is favorably positioned. At the beginning of July and the beginning of August, we see Jupiter transiting Mars/Saturn, and Jupiter is therefore in an unfavorable cosmic condition. Uranus path is nearly parallel to the midpoint Saturn/Moon's Node. Just as the cosmic condition of the positions is examined in the cosmogram, the cosmic condition of the transiting planets is also to be seen from the midpoint ephemeris.

Books available in English language

Reinhold Ebertin
THE COMBINATION OF STELLAR INFLUENCES
has been available for 15 years in English. This book contains, in addition to a short introduction to the method, 1117 examples or combinations for all aspects and midpoints. The short and precise examples differ fundamentally from the ambiguous rules of most handbooks.

RAPID AND RELIABLE ANALYSIS
After an introduction into the Ebertin method, the author shows numerous examples and drawings of how the essential elements of a cosmogram can be immediately recognized and how various dispositions manifest or become acute. There are examples of successful people and the single stages of success as shown in their cosmograms. This book also treats the constellations of radical change in the way of life, the configurations of peril in sportsmen, and examples of human failure. In addition to the book's 20 detailed examples, many other brief examples are given.

Dr. Theodor Landscheidt
COSMIC CYBERNETICS
The Foundations of a modern Astrology
In German speaking countries, Dr. Landscheidt is a well known and a leading figure in the field of fundamental astrological research. His talks given at the "Work Congresses for Cosmobiological Research" have been revolutionary in spirit and content. To the English speaking world this book serves as an introduction of the ideas of this prominent researcher.

TABLES OF EVENTS
facilitate the calculation of the solar arc directions. By a simple fundamental calculation it is possible to specify the individual solar arc for every year of life. This method is of great help when correcting the birth-time.

AUXILIARY TABLES FOR THE CALCULATION OF STELLAR POSITIONS
These tables specify the differences in daily movement exactly up to 5 minutes and facilitate the calculation of the stellar positions. This way is quicker than calculating with logarithms.

FIXED STARS AND THEIR INTERPRETATION
A useful work and a great help for any researcher and expert.

MAN IN THE UNIVERSE

In this book, Reinhold Ebertin gives an introductory view of astrological history and its evolution into modernday cosmobiology. The book also outlines various working methods such as the casting of a natal chart and the evaluation of its elements, finding out the midpoints and structural pictures and setting up the proper interpretations from these, the systematic application of the Graphic Ephemerides and other supplementary techniques.